"In this short and enc_____
most in our fight aga_____
rejoice as I read abou_____
delivers with solid Bibl_____ truth and practical ideas for fighting sin
and temptation."

Paul Worcester, Director of Christian Challenge at Chico
State, author of *Tips for Starting A College Ministry*, and coauthor of
The Fuel and The Flame: Igniting Your College Campus For Jesus Christ

"This short book comes densely packed with a biblical arsenal
for the fight against entrenched sin. Those with the courage to take
to heart what they find here will find much to help them toward
the glory of their Lord and Savior Jesus Christ."

Peter Krol, President of DiscipleMakers campus ministry
and author of *Knowable Word: Helping Ordinary People Learn to Study
the Bible*

"This book will be a treasure for anyone who knows that the
battle against sin can't be won by merely digging deeper into one's
own resolve. Andy reminds readers to instead dig deeper into Jesus
for the rest and motivation to fight relentlessly. I was helped and
you will be too."

Chase Abner, Founding member of Collegiate Collective

"I've had this question in my mind for a lot of years. Why is it
that some Christ-followers seem to experience substantial victory
over sin and others seem to consistently struggle, feeling defeated,
discouraged and disappointed over their lack of progress?

Andy Cimbala in his new book, *"The Relentless Fight,"* gives us
excellent insight on this critical topic. The book is gospel centered,
gospel driven and offers solid help for all of us in our battle against
the enemy of our souls. Andy takes the promise of victory we find
in Romans 6, shares his own experiences and journey and offers us
hope which we so desperately need and want.

By His grace and the power of the Holy Spirit, we can lay
aside every weight, and the sin which clings so closely and run
with endurance the race that is set before us as we look to Jesus -

I

Hebrews 12:1,2. Andy will model and explain how victory can be a reality. I am encouraged by the book and believe you will be too."

Dave Kraft, Life/Leadership Coach, Author of *Leaders Who Last*

"This book is raw, honest, theological, yet practical. Andy reflects on some of the best resources around and creates a practical resource that could be used by anyone."

Rashard Barnes, Groups and Connections Pastor at Mercy Church, writer for Collegiate Collective

"I remember being in college, broken over my sin and looking for hope — what a grace this book would have been! *"The Relentless Fight"* is God-glorifying, gospel-focused, biblically-saturated, and clearly practical! As someone who now works with college students, this will become my go-to resource for aiding the church in the relentless fight against sin."

T. L. Callison, Mobilizer with The Traveling Team

"The Relentless Fight is an honest, gut-wrenching look into the soul of a sincere believer who desperately wants to be free of sin and bondage. God shows him the way to victory...and He can show you too."

Steve Shadrach, Founder of Student Mobilization, Author of *The Fuel and the Flame*

"Many books have been written about how to fight and overcome sin of all sorts. *The Relentless Fight* takes on this topic in one of the most concise and applicable ways I've seen yet. Andy's heart for college students comes out clearly in the book. Its value isn't limited only to college students, though. I found the book immediately applicable and shared the core principles with a friend who needed to hear exactly what Andy had written. I know this book will be helpful to me and I expect this book will be helpful to many others as well."

Mike Puckett, e3 Partners and the #NoPlaceLeft Coalition

"This book is a must-read for every believer if they long to fight sin. While Andy talks about sex and lust mainly, the strategy he prescribes is useful for fighting any sin. You will not be able to put this small book down. This is the first book I have read that teaches you to fight *from* your identity instead of fighting *for* your identity."

Antonio D. Morton Jr, Campus Ministry Staff at Shippensburg University with Coalition for Christian Outreach (CCO) in partnership with Shippensburg First Church of God

"This book is relentlessly honest about sexual sin and relentlessly hopeful about the gospel. Those disillusioned in their quest for purity will meet in these pages a veteran that has been humbled on the battlefield of lust and yet has survived to tell us about the victory Jesus always brings."

David Kieffer, Associate Pastor of Adult Ministries at Westminster Presbyterian Church, Lancaster PA

"One of the things I enjoyed most about this book was Andy's authentic honesty about his personal battles and the process of healing and growth God took him through to live in obedient surrender.

The Relentless Fight is a helpful reminder for every believer to remember that in the war against sin we fight from victory not for victory. Beloved "Christ has already won! This means we are always fighting a defeated enemy."

Curtis Dunlap, Family Life and Teaching Pastor at Epiphany Fellowship Church, Philadelphia, PA

"Sin and the relentless guilt and shame it causes are a troubling plague for many young people. Andy's book offers healing, help, and hope through the power of the cross! This is a book that offers freedom beyond your past— into the future destiny God has for you."

Josiah Kennealy, Pastor at Minnesota Young Adults, Author of *Debtless*

THE RELENTLESS FIGHT

THE POWER OF THE GOSPEL IN THE FIGHT AGAINST SIN

ANDY CIMBALA

TABLE OF CONTENTS

INTRO: READ THIS FIRST

"Do you mortify; do you make it your daily work; be always at it while you live; cease not a day from this work; be killing sin or it will be killing you." – John Owen, The Mortification of Sin[1]

****

I pray that God uses this short book to encourage, empower, and equip you in your fight against sin. As an introduction, let me explain four things: the gospel, the core idea of this book, who should read it, and why.

The Gospel

Whatever power this book has, that power is from the gospel of Jesus Christ, applied to your heart by the work of the Holy Spirit.

What is the gospel? It's the good news that "Christ died for our sins" (1 Corinthians 15:3). We were created by God to worship Him, but we rebelled and worshiped His creation instead (Romans 1). We were meant to be in joyful relationship with our God, but instead we abandoned and rejected Him. The consequence for that sinful rebellion is death and hell; and our greatest danger is the just and holy wrath of God against us. We stand condemned and without hope, spiritually dead and morally depraved.

But God loved us and wanted a different ending to our story! So He sent Jesus to the earth on a mission. He lived the perfect life that we should have. He died the death we deserved and guaranteed our redemption. He satisfied the wrath of God by His sacrifice of atonement on the cross. The gospel is the power of God for salvation (Romans 1:16). It's the demonstration of God's love for us (Romans 5:8). It's the offer that God makes to forgive our sins and transform our lives. It's the only hope for victory over our besetting sins. The gospel is the solution to our problem of slavery to sin and being under God's deserved wrath. Without the gospel we remain condemned by God and stuck with our sin (John 3:36). The gospel is central in this book, and must be central in our lives.

The Core Idea

Let me give you the core idea at the front of the book. In our fight against our besetting sins we are prone to intense discouragement. This discouragement leaves us vulnerable to forget the good news of our forgiveness in Christ and to stop fighting. How should we respond to this temptation to give up? The main point of this book is two recommended steps, and they are pretty simple:

1. Remember the gospel.
2. Keep fighting.

If you remember the gospel, you will fight your sin. But you won't keep fighting sin unless you first remember the gospel; it's like an engine with no gas, the gospel is the fuel. *So the order is vitally important: gospel first.* **Remember the gospel. Keep fighting. That is The Relentless Fight.**

Who Should Read This?

I wrote this book for struggling sinners like me. What is sin? Sin is any transgression of God's law (1 John 3:4), it is anytime we love or value or worship anything above God (Romans i). I wrote this book for those who fight besetting sins, addictions, deep struggles, and persistent idolatries. For me one particular struggle is lust & sexual sin. But the content in this book can be applied with any kind of besetting sins, not just sexual sins. Whether you struggle with food, money, sports, drugs, academics, TV shows, alcohol, porn, disordered sexuality, gossip, pride, gambling, shopping, approval, social media, ministry, or any other good or bad thing that has taken the place of God in your life... this book is for you. Depending on your struggle, you may benefit from more professional help, beyond the scope of this short book. I'm not a licensed counselor, therapist, or psychiatrist; so I can't give professional diagnosis or prescription. I'm just a struggling Christian, speaking to other struggling Christians, pointing us both to Jesus.

If you've been struggling with persistent sin, you're probably frustrated. You might be angry. You feel alone. You may be feeling discouraged, scared that you're never going to change, terrified that this might be the last straw and God won't forgive you for the thousandth failure. You most likely feel defeated and ready to give up.

But I assume that you want to fight this thing. I assume you're sick and tired of defeat. You've been fighting for a while but you're so discouraged that you feel like throwing in the towel. Keep reading. Brother, sister, I wrote this for you. I know that same dark pit, and there is a way out. *There is hope.*

However, it is possible that someone asked you to read this book, and maybe you know you need to change, but you just don't want to or aren't ready. That's understandable. I encourage you to keep reading and pray that God would change your heart and give you motivation to fight your sin. It can feel overwhelming, but consider that God has you reading this book, in this moment. Perhaps this is your next step.

Why Read It?

I wrote this book to *help* people like me. The content was born out of my own deep struggles with sin, so my prayer is that God may use the failures, victories, and lessons learned in my life to give you hope. Have I arrived? Am I the guru? No. I'm struggling, striving, and violently pursuing holiness, beset by weakness and failure, just like you! It's good to have some companions for the journey.

I'm praying that God uses this short book to help you in *your* fight, whatever sin it is. I'm praying that God will **encourage** you by knowing that you are not alone, that He will **empower** you with the hope of the gospel, and that He will **equip** you with practical strategies for fighting your sin. Let's begin.

CHAPTER 1: SEX WAS MY GOD

"...for my people have committed two evils: they have forsaken me, the fountain of living waters, and hewed out cisterns for themselves, broken cisterns that can hold no water." – Jeremiah 2:13

****

God gets all the glory for the story of my life. I'm a sinner saved by grace.

Christian Upbringing

I grew up in a conservative evangelical Christian household. I had all the markings of a good church kid. I beat all the other kids at Bible Drills. I was confirmed and baptized in the church. I memorized the Sermon on the Mount as a requirement to get my driver's permit. I attended Christian summer camps. I went to Christian school. Christian youth group. Christian concerts. Christian novels. Christian T-shirts. Christian language, life, culture, friends, and family.

I also was enslaved to pornography. Sex was my god.

First Fruits of Sexual Sin

My curiosity with sex went back to at least late elementary school; I remember intensely reading the encyclopedia's entry on "sex" in 5th grade, and getting caught by my parents at Barnes & Noble in the sex section, soaking up the images with curious eyes. By the time my parents had "the sex talk" with me, I told them I knew it all and didn't have any questions. I remember the first time I read about masturbation in a prominent Christian author's book for teenagers. He said it was fine, every guy did it, but just don't do it too much. So I tried it. *And I loved it.* What started out as a curious experiment soon became a regular pleasurable habit. It was one of my favorite activities and my cure for boredom.

My lust quickly progressed to buying rated-R movies and hiding them, until one day I saw my first pornographic video. I was over at my friend's house, and he had porn in the VCR. So as we were playing video games one moment, then somebody pressed play, and instead of a digital machine gun, I saw something far more exciting. From that point on, *I was hooked.* I had never felt so alive, such a rush! I wanted *more* of this. It was exhilarating, yet also shameful; I knew inherently it was wrong, but I couldn't stop thinking about it. More pleasurable than any experience of masturbation, *I loved porn.* And porn combined with the rush of a masturbated orgasm? *Addictive.*

Soon after that the Internet exploded in popularity. People talked about "surfing the web" and a ton of file-sharing services started up. So during the week I'd download porn; I made sure to cover my tracks and write everything to floppy disks which I hid in my room. Late at night I'd sneak out into the living room to watch porn. I loved my sin, but also instinctively hid it, and fiercely protected it. I felt guilty for lying and hiding, but that guilt didn't lead to repentance. I knew somewhere in my heart that porn was a sin, but I didn't do much to fight it.

It was so exhilarating! And shameful. I hated it... but I loved it more.

Andy: The Sex Guy

Sex Ed in 9th grade was my favorite class. I made jokes, carefully studied the material, and eagerly awaited 11th grade when we would go even more in-depth. But by 11th grade I had already started to branch out on my own, studying books and reading up on the topic. I wasn't the best at any other area in school: music, academics, sports, popularity, or wealth. But I desperately wanted just *one* thing that I could be the best at. I wanted one arena where I would win every time. I wanted something that I could be known for, something I could stake my identity on. And I chose sex. I quickly realized that most people were ashamed and squirmy about sexuality. And if I just read a few more things than they did, and was able to talk about it without blushing, I would have an advantage over every other person in the school. This could be the identity that I had longed for! So I went for it. I became Andy: The Sex Guy; giving out sexual advice, asking people about their experiences, recommending techniques, learning all I could, and advertising myself as the sex-answers man. I was reading any books I could get my hands on, asking questions and stumping my health teacher, and by the end of high school I had even visited the local college library and had read several college-level books. I was serious. I took notes, scanned pages, began assembling my resource library, and started looking into making sexual education and therapy my academic career.

Back in high school as I started to form my identity around sex, it was a joke among my friends, "haha, Andy, you're such a pervert..." But as I entered college, I realized that I could become serious in my pursuit of sexuality as an academic discipline. I could actually *make* sex my real identity. And so I did.

College: Feeding the Idol

In college, you have a buffet of academic options and social identities: Who will you be? What will you be known for? What clubs will you join? What accolades will you strive after? As I entered that new world of college at Penn State, I knew exactly what I would pick to focus on: sex.

I made this commitment as I began summer classes in 2004, and then had the opportunity to solidify this vision in the fall semester. I was meeting with my academic advisor, eagerly explaining to him my plans for an undergraduate degree in (probably) psychology. Ultimately I had planned to go on to grad school to get my masters, my PhD, and then live my dream. I was excited to teach sex at a university, write books about sex, do sex counseling, lead research on sex, and transform the world of sex education. I was on fire, and consumed by my grand vision of sex.

I was surprised when my advisor informed me about a program within the College of Liberal Arts called Letters, Arts, & Sciences that allowed me to create my *own* custom major if my academic goals were not able to be satisfied by a preexisting major. This was music to my ears! "I can do that?" I asked incredulously, "Then sign me up!" I got the paperwork and started ferociously writing my proposal. I talked with professors around campus, I researched classes online, and I quickly crafted my own custom major about sex. A few weeks later emerged *my* major, "Biopsychosocial Aspects of Sexuality," and I was thrilled at my own accomplishment. No one else had it; it was my own custom creation. It was another sacrifice of worship and affection on the altar to the god of sex. And I couldn't have been happier.

That first fall semester at Penn State I had 19 credits and yet I *still* found the time to read over 20 extra books on the side about sex. I was ravenous, eagerly learning as much as I possibly could, cramming knowledge in my brain at a furious rate. I would look at endnotes, figure out the books that were most cross-referenced, and then order those through Inter-Library Loan, rejoicing when I got the email that they had arrived! Over the course of my years of college I studied scores of different books and resources to supplement my classes. I'd read books on the way to class, I'd read books while eating lunch, I'd carry books around on my dorm floor and try to educate my floormates with whatever current material I was learning. I was a passionate sex-evangelist!

And with each book that I read, I filled my mind with knowledge. But more importantly, I filled my heart with *pride*. Nobody knew as much as me, and that's exactly what I wanted. Even one professor commented that I knew more about sex than her. Ah, that was what my prideful heart most wanted to hear. I wanted to be the best. I pursued sex academically, but also practically. I was trying to learn sexual techniques to maximize my sexual fulfillment. I was experimenting and training, like an athlete. These sex manuals were my Bible, masturbation was my worship, and sex was my religion.

Christian Sexual Ethics

Let's briefly pause my story to talk about Christian sexual ethics. I don't know what comes to your mind when you hear the words "porn" and "masturbation." For many typical Americans, they believe these things are no big deal, everybody does it at some point, and they certainly aren't sinful. Perhaps you're reading this and you wouldn't identify as a Christian. Or maybe you grew up going to church but you're confused about what the Bible says. Perhaps you know what the Bible teaches, but you don't agree. But increasingly, even secular thinkers are recognizing the ill effects of pornography in our society. Fight the New Drug[2] is a recent example of a non-religious organization that seeks to raise awareness of the negative fruits of porn: fueling sex trafficking, warping perceptions of human bodies, changing the brain, and becoming addictive. In a sense, the secular culture is catching up to what the Bible has already been saying for centuries.

In the Bible, God defines and condemns sexual sin; repeatedly we are exhorted to pursue sexual purity and to avoid sexual immorality. God created sex, and as its Creator He has a lot to say about sexual ethics. Perhaps the clearest example is Jesus speaking in Matthew 5:27-29, "You have heard that it was said, 'You shall not commit adultery.' But I say to you that everyone who looks at a woman with lustful intent has already committed adultery with her in his heart. If your right eye causes you to sin, tear it out and throw it away. For it is better that you lose one of your members than that your whole body be thrown into hell." Jesus uses some of the harshest possible language and warning against sexual lust and sin. Kill this sin! Or be thrown into hell. Yikes. Yet Jesus' strong exhortation is in harmony with the rest of the Scripture's teaching on sexual ethics.[3]

Pornography is a sin. It is a grievous rebellion against God and a perversion of His good creation of sex. Pornography is the centerpiece of my testimony. But the sin of pornography might not be your specific struggle, perhaps you're fighting another besetting sin like idolatry of food or money or academics or alcohol. Whatever your struggle, I trust you can relate as I tell my story. Let's jump back in.

Living Hypocrisy

That whole first year of college was also a year of strange hypocrisy; I was outwardly religious but inwardly immoral. Since I had grown up in the church, I had in the back of my mind that a Christian in college should be involved in some kind of college ministry, just like youth group in high school. So I got involved in a Christian club, went to Bible study, large group meeting, even was discipled by an older guy my whole freshman year. My Dad picked me up every Sunday morning to faithfully attend my parents' church. But there was a deep disconnect: I loved sex more than Jesus. My identity was built around sexuality instead of the God who created sex. Sex was in the center, and Jesus was on the periphery. On a Friday afternoon I'd be dispersing sexual advice and recommendations to as many as would come and listen. And then in the evening I'd go to the Christian large group meeting and sing worship songs to Jesus. I worshipped sex in the afternoon, and then worshipped Jesus in the evening, and then worshipped sex again with porn when I went back to my dorm later at night. My outer shell was distinctly Christian, while my inner core was increasingly idolatrous of sex. This was a massive problem! I had rejected God in my heart and affections, while still holding on to the vestiges of religion in my schedule and attendance. God calls this evil in Jeremiah 2:13, "…for my people have committed two evils: they have forsaken me, the fountain of living waters, and hewed out cisterns for themselves, broken cisterns that can hold no water." I was like the ancient Israelites that God condemned in Isaiah 29:13, quoted by Jesus in Matthew 15:7-9 against the Pharisees, "This people honors me with their lips, but their heart is far from me." I was a textbook hypocrite, but I didn't even know it. This kind of hypocrisy is so dangerous, because it is blinding.

Starting the Fight: Realizing I'm a Sinner

That was my freshman year of college: filled with scores of books, countless hours of pornography, masturbation, lustful fantasy, and worship of the god of sex. But God began something in me even that spring semester. I began to pray and more regularly write out my prayers to God in a green spiral-bound journal, and I began to read the Bible more. Looking back, I believe prayer and Bible reading were the catalyst for further change. During the summer of 2005, after my freshman year, I continued classes at Penn State. Living in a single dorm alone on campus, with no Christian friends and no accountability, I looked at porn more than ever. But something significant changed in my heart. Something only God could do. That summer, although I did *look* at porn, there was one life-changing difference that began to arise: *I didn't want to look anymore.* I don't know how it happened, and I can't pinpoint one special day, but the Holy Spirit began slowly changing my heart. My prayer journal entries from that time reflect a growing hatred of sin, a more fervent crying out for deliverance and freedom, and prayers for God to strengthen me by showing me His love. The hypocritical disconnect of living a double life had begun to crack. See, there's an awful tension you feel when you have to live two parallel lives, but the pain of hypocrisy is often less than the pain of living authentically. If you merge your two lives to be an authentic person, it means directly confronting the sins of your hidden life, and without the power of the gospel the exposure is unbearable. Without Jesus being more lovely, you won't ever kill the sin you love.[4] God began to thread this needle, and the big first step was sexual holiness.

For the first time in my life, I started **struggling** with porn, instead of hiding and protecting it. I confessed it to the Lord, I tried to stop, I prayed for God to bring change. The Holy Spirit of God was at work in my heart, growing in me the first-fruits of repentance! It's like He began a slow-burn increase in my desire for obedience, which eventually overtook my desire for sin, which slowly resulted in changed behavior. I read a book called *Not Even a Hint: Guarding Your Heart Against Lust*[5] and it gave me a new desire to fight my sin. What I encountered that summer as I struggled to fight against pornography was the unbelievable *strength* of this lust that I had worked so hard to cultivate. The god of sex was strong in my life. Sex was on the throne, and was *not* going to leave without a fight. But Jesus was bigger.

As a counter-attack, I began to consume huge quantities of the Word of God. From my Christian upbringing, I knew this was my key weapon in the fight (Ephesians 6:17). I started carrying a pocket Bible with me around campus, and as I would walk to class or wait in line or eat my lunch I would be reading the New Testament instead of books about sex. What a change! I prayed and journaled and poured out my heart to God. The guilt I had been suppressing for years was now functioning properly: it was driving me to the cross in confession and prayer. My guilt was showing me my need for a Savior.

And then one day, the Lord broke through in a dramatic way. In a swift act of repentance, I threw out a large amount of sexual material. I just threw it in the trash can down the hall from my room, as an act of turning my back on this god of sex, to worship the true God: Jesus Christ. This was a milestone. Like the Israelites in the Old Testament, I was tearing down the Asherah poles, breaking apart the altars to Baal, and returning to the LORD God.[6] For what felt like the first time in my life…I was repenting.

Growth through DiscipleMakers

Around this time, I realized that I *needed* Christian community. I couldn't do this on my own! I was weak, and I needed help. Christianity is a *team* sport! In order to fight my sin, and to grow spiritually, I needed challenge. I needed to get some serious Bible study. I needed discipleship and accountability. And in God's grace, He provided abundantly.

Walking to lunch one day in Pollock Commons, I passed by an info table with Bibles on it. Excitedly, I stopped and asked, "Do you guys do Bible studies?" It was an outreach table hosted by a Christian student club that was still active on campus that summer, when most ministries take a break until the start of fall classes. I eagerly signed up for more info with DiscipleMakers Christian Fellowship, and was soon contacted by staff worker David Royes. We grabbed lunch at Burger King, where in prideful church-kid fashion I grilled him with questions, seeing if he was the real deal. I wanted challenge! So I asked him what kind of Bible studies they had available in the summer? Here was his answer: a study in Ecclesiastes, at 7am on Saturday mornings, a 15-minute walk from my dorm, led by a guy who graduated from Harvard and knew Hebrew and Greek. This was the challenge I was looking for.

I attended this summer Bible study and met up again with David a few times. When the fall semester of 2005 started, I jumped into this new community eagerly. I really wanted to change! I wanted to be rid of that double life and really grow in Christian maturity, and I knew I needed help from others. I met with David regularly, and he challenged me in all areas of my life by bringing me to the Scriptures. I joined an intensive men's Bible study through the gospel of John. I got on board with a new initiative called the Leadership Team, which was a group of students committed to starting outreach Bible studies in their dorms.

During that fall semester I attended a state-wide conference that DiscipleMakers hosted, and bought a book at their booktable called *Sex and the Supremacy of Christ*, which was a compilation of sessions from the 2004 Desiring God National Conference. It included a DVD of the two main sessions by John Piper. I was confused by the title of the book. Wasn't sex the best? How could Christ be supreme over sex? This confusion showed the vestiges of my idolatry of sex. Even though I had begun many steps of repentance, the god of sex was still clawing to stay on the throne. But I watched those sermons, again and again. And I was blown away. Never before had I heard anyone preach like that. Never before had I heard such an exalted view of Jesus Christ. Piper preached on the supremacy of Christ in His deity, eternality, constancy, knowledge, wisdom, authority, providence, word, purity, trustworthiness, justice, patience, obedience, meekness, wrath, grace, love, and gladness.[7] Was Jesus truly supreme and sovereign and superior over everything? Was He really that big? Piper goes on to conclude, "Knowing the supremacy of Christ enlarges the soul so that sex and its little thrills become as small as they really are."[8] Was sex really that small in comparison? A deep change began to happen in my heart. It was that fall semester when I first wrote in my prayer journal, "Sex is not that big of a deal," as I was realizing that God was bigger. My identity was beginning to shift from sex to Jesus. He was increasingly regaining His rightful place at the center of my life.

As I looked back on that school year, I was shocked at the changes that God was doing in my life. It would seem that every *week* He was teaching me something new and radical. Christian language and words that I had known for years like "sin, gospel, repentance, faith" suddenly had new depth and relevance in my life! The Scriptures were opening up to me in ways they never had before. And as the months progressed, I began to understand the gospel for perhaps the first time: I was a sinner, Christ died in my place, I can be forgiven and live a new life, I am called to be a disciple and to make disciples. This was *big*!

Vision Shift

In summer 2006, I did an internship with DiscipleMakers, and it was life-changing. I was participating in fruitful ministry, and was being challenged about my worldview and life-mission. What was I living for? What would I do after graduation? What would I give my life to?

Joel Martin, my DiscipleMakers mentor for the summer, asked me a significant question, "How do you change the world?" As I considered this seemingly easy question, I realized that I didn't have my usual easy answer. Previously, I would have answered "education" and begin to argue my points from my sex major. But now that I had seen the power of discipleship in my life, the answer had changed. Now that I had seen the command from Jesus to make disciples (Matthew 28:18-20), the answer had changed. Now that I had participated in investing in other folks for their spiritual growth, the answer had changed. "How do you change the world?" Joel asked. I responded, "You do what Jesus did: you invest in a few, who reach the many. You make disciples."

It worked for Jesus, it has worked for the last 2,000 years of Christian history, and it is still our calling today.

Putting it into my own words was the turning point. If that were true, was I really living like that? My life needed to change in a big way. I applied to be on staff with DiscipleMakers; after graduation, I would devote my life to making disciples of Jesus Christ!

I experienced a big shift that summer: the god of sex came down from the throne. Jesus Christ toppled it. It had no business as god of my life! Jesus retook His rightful throne, ruling and reigning in His supremacy. And I couldn't have been happier.

The Relentless Fight

I wish I could end the story here, saying that victory was my daily joy from then on. Sadly, the fight was only beginning. What I experienced was a slow and steady process of sanctification. I thought the struggle would be easy, fast, and clean. But instead it was a hard, long, bloody fight.[9] I read all the books and resources I could get, but still I struggled. There were some occasional victories. Lustful thoughts were easier to fight now. There were some weeks where I made a conscious choice to *not* look at porn even when *everything* in me was screaming to do it. Those were powerful decisions of faith, choosing to trust that God's Word was true, despite all my feelings to the contrary. Those times were big victories over my god of sex. They were so painful, so difficult; to say no felt like death. I was carving a new path, seeking to depart from a well-worn years-old habit. But each victory was evidence to me that Jesus Christ was the One on the throne, and He was slowly advancing on every part of my life. He was bringing victory and freedom as His grace and love reigned supreme. It was hard-fought progress. But still the struggle dragged on, and I failed with pornography and masturbation every few weeks. This filled me with guilt, shame, anger, frustration, discouragement, sadness, and a fear that I would never change. Tragically, this toxic mixture of feelings would sometimes drive me back to pornography again as an anesthetic. Thus the vicious cycle continued: fail, try hard to be more disciplined, fail, try harder, fail, feel so bad and want to give up but try again just a little bit, fail. Do you know what it does to a person, to fail and fail and fail and fail repeatedly? It breaks your spirit. Persistent failure shreds your hope and replaces it with discouragement. And nothing guts your soul like pornography. It eviscerates the soul. And so my life was binge, purge, binge, purge... the vicious cycle dragged on. This was *years*. It was a brutal battle.

It was in the midst of this struggle, this discouragement, and this agony, that The Relentless Fight was born. I was wildly hungry for hope. I was so discouraged, so defeated by each failure. Then this God-given realization rang in my life like a bell: **I didn't need a new strategy, or a new book, or a new sermon, or just doing things better, or *more*, or trying harder...but I needed a *Savior*.** And that was *precisely* what Jesus Christ had provided for me in the gospel!! Wonder of wonders! My greatest need had already been fully provided! I began to fight in a completely different way: I made it my *first* response to launch a fierce, all-out war to remember the gospel. *After* that, I would re-engage the fight against sin by strategies and tactics and trying harder. But the fight wasn't about hard work, powered by my own self-will or ability. The fight was about Christ's work, powered by the *gospel*. The good news of the gospel means it didn't matter how much I failed, I was loved and accepted by God because of the atonement of Jesus. And yet that love and acceptance and forgiveness motivated me to fight my sin!

This was a paradigm that I hadn't found in any book or resource: *remember the gospel,* **then** *keep fighting.* It was so exciting! My biggest need was already provided for: forgiveness from my terrible sin. This forgiveness motivated me to fight, unlike the guilt and shame and fear that accompanied my failure. How could I endure when I felt so defeated? What could keep me going in the midst of such a difficult fight? How could I keep fighting when I kept failing? The answer filled me with such joy and power: *the gospel of Jesus Christ.* He died for me, that I might live for Him. Glory to God!

****

How can we endure in the fight? How do we respond to failures? How does the gospel change our perspective and motivate us? Let's dive into all this and more. But first, let's be real about where we all start: in a place of deep discouragement.

CHAPTER 2: DISCOURAGEMENT AND LIES

"How long, O Lord? Will you forget me forever? How long will you hide your face from me? How long must I take counsel in my soul and have sorrow in my heart all the day? How long shall my enemy be exalted over me?" – Psalm 13:1-2

****

Are you discouraged? Are you utterly exhausted by your own sin? Do you feel ready to give up, so discouraged that you don't even have the strength to pray? Are you so sick and tired of having to confess the same sins to God, that you're just *done* confessing? (I mean, what's the point? You're just going to fail again anyway...)

Are you terrified to share this with someone else? Do you feel alone? As if no one else understands your struggle, and you have no help in the fight? Do you feel like you don't actually have anyone to rely on, that basically...you're on your own? Maybe you reach out to a few brothers or sisters, but nobody texts you back. Well, at least you tried. (Guess you really are on your own...)

Do you feel condemned? Do you feel attacked? Do you hear accusations in the back of your mind? Perhaps you feel and hear, "You are a failure. You are dirty. You are an addict. You will never change. You will never get free. You are pathetic. You are worthless. You are weak." Is Satan feeding you these lies? Do you hear untruths spoken about God? Maybe you hear, "He won't forgive you. He's tired of you. He is so ashamed of you. He's against you. He's disgusted by you. He hates you."

This is the experience of discouragement and lies.

In this midst of this suffocating discouragement, we become susceptible to lies, which open us up to two key temptations:

Temptation #1: Forget the Gospel: We are tempted to revert to a performance-based relationship with God, instead of remembering and believing the glorious good news that we are loved and forgiven. When we forget the gospel, we wallow in immense guilt because of our failure, thinking that God won't forgive us again *this* time. When we forget the gospel, we have no power to change, and we are consumed with shame for our dirtiness. When we forget the gospel, we have no hope anymore.

Temptation #2: Stop Fighting: Once we forget the gospel, we are then tempted to just give up. "Meh, it's not worth it, I just keep losing. What's the point?" So we slack on confessing our sin to the Lord. We start to become hardened in our sin. We no longer confess our sin with other Christians. We no longer resist it, and inevitably we come right back to the same sin. We stop fighting. We just go with the rapid current of our sinful culture and our own sinful hearts. We become vulnerable to any temptation Satan throws at us. We have lost that spark in our eyes. We've truly been defeated.

"Forget the gospel and stop fighting." This is the motto of discouragement and lies. What we *should* do is remember the gospel and keep fighting. But it makes sense that Satan would undermine our faith in the gospel. The gospel is our greatest glory and power. Satan's goal isn't necessarily to get us to commit immense soul-destroying sins (little sins are just as damning[10]). Rather, Satan's biggest goal is to get us to forget the good news of Christ's rescue and forgiveness. He knows if he can make us forget that, we're lost. If we forget the gospel, of course we'll stop fighting! We have no more power. We have no hope.

I remember some days I would fail with pornography, and be in such a discouraged state. I would feel frustrated, guilty, sad, angry...and I would often return *on that very same day* and look at porn as my twisted comfort. Why? Because I was forgetting the gospel. If I felt that I had "blown it" for the day, then that day was already a failure; I was a failure, so why even try anymore? And what could I do with all this guilt? I guess just look at porn again, that usually made me anesthetized for a few minutes. This became a vicious cycle; sin begets more sin when the gospel is forgotten. I would throw myself into a binging of sin because of my deep sense of defeat and hopelessness. I would often think, "There's no use even trying." This is the fruit of forgetting the gospel.

Can you relate to this discouragement? In the struggle with sin, are you susceptible to debilitating lies? How do you respond to this incredibly heavy weight of guilt and shame? What is our lifeline to grab onto before we completely sink in this quicksand? What do we do with our discouragement? How do we combat the lies that undermine our faith? How do we endure amidst such difficulty? Answer: we must make war! We must *relentlessly fight* to remember the gospel.

CHAPTER 3: WHAT IS THE GOSPEL?

"Set faith at work on Christ for the killing of your sin. His blood is the great sovereign remedy for sin-sick souls. Live in this, and you will die a conqueror; yea, you will, through the good providence of God, live to see your lust dead at your feet." – John Owen, The Mortification of Sin [11]

****

The gospel is the most amazing news in the world! The gospel proves God's love for us, and empowers us to live new transformed lives that honor God. The gospel displays to us the horror of our sin, and the beauty of our God. The gospel instills dynamic joy in our hearts. The gospel is the means of God reconciling us back to Himself, so that we can have joy and life in His presence. The gospel is the grounds for our assurance of forgiveness. The gospel grants to us the indwelling of the Holy Spirit, who not only helps to kill our sin, but helps to make us holy.

But what is the gospel? Let's make sure we're on the same page about this glorious power.

What is the Gospel?

The word "gospel" simply means "good news." The gospel is not merely good advice from a self-help guru. It is the very good *news* of what Christ has accomplished for us. And it is remarkably *good* news!

One of my favorite passages in the Bible is 1 Corinthians 15:1-4, because it's the simplest definition of the gospel, and Paul writes clearly of the gospel's supremacy and importance. Let's take a closer look and do some Bible study:

"1 Now I would remind you, brothers, of the gospel I preached to you, which you received, in which you stand, 2 and by which you are being saved, if you hold fast to the word I preached to you—unless you believed in vain. 3 For I delivered to you as of first importance what I also received: that Christ died for our sins in accordance with the Scriptures, 4 that he was buried, that he was raised on the third day in accordance with the Scriptures..."

Look at verse 1. These Christians already know the gospel! And yet Paul desires to *remind* them of what they already know. Isn't that surprising? It's the same gospel he had already preached to them, it's the same gospel they had previously received, and it's the same gospel they are currently standing in. And yet Paul desires to remind them "of the gospel I preached to you." They need to remember the gospel.

Look at verse 2. There is a progressive salvation happening by the power of this gospel. They are *being* saved by this gospel, it's an ongoing process. But then Paul adds, "if." If they don't hold fast to that word, then their belief is in vain. They have to endure! It won't do them any good to hear it, believe it once, but then move on and forget it. They have to remember the gospel.

Finally, look at verse 3. Paul gave the gospel to the Corinthians, "as of *first* importance," as the most significant thing that he told them when he was first physically present with them. Now that he's absent, he's giving it to them again in a letter, because it's so important. The more important something is, the more we feel the need to repeat ourselves! He wants them to hold fast to the gospel.

What is that gospel? Paul goes on in the next verses with a few more details, but I'd like to focus on the five-word summary he writes in verse 3: "Christ died for our sins." Wow. Just five words, but there is so much packed in here. "Christ died for our sins." Let's slow it down and take each word one at a time:

Christ: The man who died is *Christ*, the Messiah, the incarnate Word of God. The second person of the Trinity, the One who commands the dead to be alive, who walks on water, and tells the wind to stop. This is Jesus of Nazareth; He was the only human who lived a perfect life.

Died: This One, He *died*. Though He was innocent and undeserving of death, He was stripped naked, nailed to a Roman cross, and publicly executed as a common criminal. His life was extinguished. He was buried in the tomb of Joseph of Arimathea.

For: This death was *for* something. It did not occur in a vacuum. It had purpose, meaning, it was intentional. It was the means to something better, something outside of just the event. This death accomplished a goal.

Our: Christ did not die for His sins, because He had no sin. Rather, He died for His people. The sins are *our* sins, the ones that we have done. This is where things get so magnificent! Christ didn't have to die for His sins, and at the same time we should have died for our sins. And yet there's this incredible exchange: We sin. He dies.

Sins: The reason why Christ had to die was for our *sins*. We have all transgressed and broken God's law. We have rebelled against His authority. We are corrupt, wicked, evil, and oppose God in His righteousness. Therefore we are under God's just wrath, we are cut off from relationship with Him, and we deserve death (Romans 6:23). But Christ was the one who took this death upon Himself, in our place, *for our sins* (2 Corinthians 5:21). This is what Christ died for. Not an example, not a political statement, and not an accident. He died as the atonement for the sins of His people.

That is the gospel, in only five words! *"Christ died for our sins."* How glorious! Because of the gospel, we have forgiveness of sins, even though we were guilty and condemned in God's courtroom. Because of the gospel, we are restored back into right relationship with our great Father God, even though our sins were a barrier and we were God's enemies. Because of the gospel, we have the power and presence of the Holy Spirit and we can now walk in holiness and freedom, even though we were dead in our sins and enslaved to impurity. The gospel is such good news!

Notice additionally that in verse 4 Christ was buried after death and *raised* back to life. The resurrection proves that God the Father was pleased with Christ's sacrifice on our behalf. The resurrection is a declaration of "Mission Accomplished!" Paul also states in verse 3 and again in verse 4 that Christ's death and resurrection were "in accordance with the Scriptures," showing that God had predicted and planned this salvation hundreds, even thousands of years previously, as recorded in the Old Testament. His plan of salvation was through the death of Christ, and this ancient plan had now succeeded.

"Christ Died For Our Sins." These five words in I Corinthians 15 are just one small sampling of the rich feast of the gospel. If you want more, check out these other Scriptures: John 3:16, Romans 3:21-26, 2 Corinthians 5:11-21, Galatians 2:15-21, Ephesians 2:1-10, Colossians 2:6-15, and Titus 3:3-7. Or if you want to go hardcore, just read all of Romans.

What Does the Gospel Give Us?

The gospel speaks directly to all of our needs as hopeless sinners in need of rescue. Jesus provides precisely what we need, He is amazingly good. Consider some of our needs and experiences, and how overwhelmingly the gospel meets us there:

Forgiveness: The gospel gives forgiveness for our guilt.

- ❖ Acts 10:43, "To him all the prophets bear witness that everyone who believes in him receives forgiveness of sins through his name."
- ❖ Colossians 1:14, "...in whom we have redemption, the forgiveness of sins."
- ❖ I John 1:9, "If we confess our sins, he is faithful and just to forgive us our sins and to cleanse us from all unrighteousness."

Cleansing: The gospel gives cleansing of our shame and a new fresh identity in Christ.

❖ Romans 6:4, "We were buried therefore with him by baptism into death, in order that, just as Christ was raised from the dead by the glory of the Father, we too might walk in newness of life."

❖ 2 Corinthians 5:17, "Therefore, if anyone is in Christ, he is a new creation. The old has passed away; behold, the new has come."

❖ 1 John 1:7, "But if we walk in the light, as he is in the light, we have fellowship with one another, and the blood of Jesus his Son cleanses us from all sin."

Freedom: The gospel gives freedom from our slavery to sin. We are granted liberation from Satan. He transforms us into slaves of righteousness, and citizens of Christ's kingdom.

❖ Romans 6 (the whole chapter), but especially v6, "We know that our old self was crucified with him in order that the body of sin might be brought to nothing, so that we would no longer be enslaved to sin." And especially v18, "...and, having been set free from sin, have become slaves of righteousness."

❖ 2 Corinthians 3:17, "Now the Lord is the Spirit, and where the Spirit of the Lord is, there is freedom."

❖ Galatians 5:1, "For freedom Christ has set us free; stand firm therefore, and do not submit again to a yoke of slavery."

❖ Colossians 1:13, "He has delivered us from the domain of darkness and transferred us to the kingdom of his beloved Son..."

Hope: The gospel gives firm hope in the midst of our discouragement.

- ❖ Romans 5:1-5, "Therefore, since we have been justified by faith, we have peace with God through our Lord Jesus Christ. Through him we have also obtained access by faith into this grace in which we stand, and we rejoice in hope of the glory of God. Not only that, but we rejoice in our sufferings, knowing that suffering produces endurance, and endurance produces character, and character produces hope, and hope does not put us to shame, because God's love has been poured into our hearts through the Holy Spirit who has been given to us."

- ❖ 1 Peter 1:3-5, "Blessed be the God and Father of our Lord Jesus Christ! According to his great mercy, he has caused us to be born again to a living hope through the resurrection of Jesus Christ from the dead, to an inheritance that is imperishable, undefiled, and unfading, kept in heaven for you, who by God's power are being guarded through faith for a salvation ready to be revealed in the last time."

Comfort: As we face suffering and sadness, the gospel gives comfort.

- ❖ Psalm 34:18, "The Lord is near to the brokenhearted and saves the crushed in spirit."

- ❖ 2 Corinthians 1:3-7, "Blessed be the God and Father of our Lord Jesus Christ, the Father of mercies and God of all comfort, who comforts us in all our affliction, so that we may be able to comfort those who are in any affliction, with the comfort with which we ourselves are comforted by God. For as we share abundantly in Christ's sufferings, so through Christ we share abundantly in comfort too. If we are afflicted, it is for your comfort and salvation; and if we are comforted, it is for your comfort, which you experience when you patiently endure the same sufferings that we suffer. Our hope for you is unshaken, for we know that as you share in our sufferings, you will also share in our comfort."

❖ 2 Thessalonians 2:16-17, "Now may our Lord Jesus Christ himself, and God our Father, who loved us and gave us eternal comfort and good hope through grace, comfort your hearts and establish them in every good work and word."

God With Us: As we face loneliness, because of the gospel God gives us His own presence.

❖ Matthew 28:18-20, "And Jesus came and said to them, 'All authority in heaven and on earth has been given to me. Go therefore and make disciples of all nations, baptizing them in the name of the Father and of the Son and of the Holy Spirit, teaching them to observe all that I have commanded you. And behold, I am with you always, to the end of the age.'"

❖ John 14:15-17, "'If you love me, you will keep my commandments. And I will ask the Father, and he will give you another Helper, to be with you forever, even the Spirit of truth, whom the world cannot receive, because it neither sees him nor knows him. You know him, for he dwells with you and will be in you.'"

- ❖ 1 Corinthians 3:16, "Do you not know that you are God's temple and that God's Spirit dwells in you?"

Grace: The gospel gives grace for our performance failure; it's not up to our ability and work and effort. We live and stand by God's grace!

- ❖ Romans 4:4-8, "Now to the one who works, his wages are not counted as a gift but as his due. And to the one who does not work but believes in him who justifies the ungodly, his faith is counted as righteousness, just as David also speaks of the blessing of the one to whom God counts righteousness apart from works: 'Blessed are those whose lawless deeds are forgiven, and whose sins are covered; blessed is the man against whom the Lord will not count his sin.'"

- ❖ Romans 11:6, "But if it is by grace, it is no longer on the basis of works; otherwise grace would no longer be grace."

- ❖ Ephesians 2:8-9, "For by grace you have been saved through faith. And this is not your own doing; it is the gift of God, not a result of works, so that no one may boast."

Love: In the face of our feelings of worthlessness or abandonment, the gospel gives us clear proof of God's great love for us!

- ❖ John 3:16, "For God so loved the world, that he gave his only Son, that whoever believes in him should not perish but have eternal life."

- ❖ Romans 5:8, "...but God shows his love for us in that while we were still sinners, Christ died for us."

❖ Ephesians 5:1-2, "Therefore be imitators of God, as beloved children. And walk in love, as Christ loved us and gave himself up for us, a fragrant offering and sacrifice to God."

❖ 1 John 3:16, "By this we know love, that he laid down his life for us, and we ought to lay down our lives for the brothers."

Acceptance, Approval, and Adoption: The gospel gives us radical acceptance through our adoption into God's family. We are not rejected, passed over, or forgotten. We move from self-sufficient orphans to beloved sons and daughters! We are approved in Christ.

❖ Romans 8:15, "For you did not receive the spirit of slavery to fall back into fear, but you have received the Spirit of adoption as sons, by whom we cry, 'Abba! Father!'"

❖ Romans 16:10, "Greet Apelles, who is approved in Christ. Greet those who belong to the family of Aristobulus." (Approved in Christ! You're no longer a failure. Your identity is now in Christ, and therefore you are approved.)

❖ Galatians 3:25-27, "But now that faith has come, we are no longer under a guardian, for in Christ Jesus you are all sons of God, through faith. For as many of you as were baptized into Christ have put on Christ."

❖ Ephesians 1:4-6, "...he chose us in him before the foundation of the world, that we should be holy and blameless before him. In love he predestined us for adoption to himself as sons through Jesus Christ, according to the purpose of his will, to the praise of his glorious grace, with which he has blessed us in the Beloved."

Wow! The gospel is big. The gospel is amazing. When we see how Christ satisfies all our needs, and makes us new creations, and loves us so deeply, it *does* encourage us. It fills us with gratitude and joy. It begins to give us power. Once we start feeling that power of the gospel, we will want to keep fighting. The fight against sin is a response to His love.

CHAPTER 4: REMEMBER THE GOSPEL

"Well, God does not mean for us to be passive. He means for us to fight the fight of faith—the fight for joy. And the central strategy is to preach the gospel to yourself. This is war. Satan is preaching for sure. If we remain passive, we surrender the field to him." – John Piper, When I Don't Desire God [12]

****

We must relentlessly fight to remember the gospel.

If you get nothing else out of this book, or if you're too discouraged to keep reading, then please do at least receive this one exhortation: Remember the gospel. Remember the gospel. Remember the gospel.

What is The Relentless Fight?

You may think that "the relentless fight" is about fighting sin. The Christian may think, "Yeah, I'm gonna fight. Fight this sin. Fight it *harder*. More accountability, more Scripture, more prayer, more books and sermons and seminars and conferences. More discipline! I'm just too weak, right? I need to be sober-minded, I need to be more vigilant, I need more boundaries or protection or something." And that fighting attitude towards sin is commendable. But it must be *secondary*. It can't be our first response! Without Jesus, all this activity is pride-fueled and spiritually powerless.

The fight is *first* about remembering the gospel. That's the most important fight! "The relentless fight" isn't the fight against sin. Not primarily. The gospel must be first. Remembering the *gospel* is the crucial victory that will turn the tide. When we're encouraged by our rich relationship with the Lord, then we'll be motivated to keep fighting because we are grateful. When we're empowered by His forgiveness and love, then we will be motivated to keep fighting these forgiven sins. When we humbly depend on Jesus as our Savior, then we fight *from* freedom instead of *for* freedom. We have to get the order right!

1. Remember the gospel.
2. Keep fighting.

It is gospel first, then the fight, in that order. God's grace, not human effort, is the secret weapon for the effective killing of sin. But we must remember it!

Refusing the Counterfeits

"Remember the gospel" is Step 1, which is the only appropriate motivation for Step 2, "keep fighting." But gospel-substitutes offer to come in the place of Step 1 and become the replacement fuel for "keep fighting." But we must hold fast to Step 1 of "Remember the gospel" and reject the substitutes. Here are examples of some "Step 1" counterfeits that we must refuse:

"You're a good person," so keep fighting. This puts the focus on self instead of Christ. For example, "You shouldn't do that, you're better than that." or "I can't let anyone know I'm struggling in this way, I'll fight it on my own." It relies upon human pride and self-righteousness, puffing you up. The reality is that you're *not* a good person, and there's no strength in yourself to continue fighting sin. We must instead focus on Jesus. We fight by the Spirit's power, Romans 8:13, "...but if by the Spirit you put to death the deeds of the body, you will live."

"You're a terrible person," so keep fighting. This also puts the focus on self instead of Christ, but it's the inverse of pride. This gospel-substitute relies on guilt and shame as the motivation to fight our sin. For example, "You are worthless. How can you continue like this? Don't you realize God hates this? You are gross. God will never forgive you. You better clean up your act." The danger of this counterfeit is that it's partially true. In reality, we really are terrible rotten sinners! But that's only the first half of the gospel, that's the bad news *only*. Yes, we are wicked, and under God's wrath. Yes, we are guilty and our sin brings shame. But that's not all! God has looked at our guilt and shame and has forgiven us and cleansed us in the cross of Jesus. Oh glorious good news! We must instead use those feelings of guilt as a springboard to drive us back to the gospel and to kneeling at the cross.[13] God promises us in 1 John 1:9, "If we confess our sins, he is faithful and just to forgive us our sins and to cleanse us from all unrighteousness."

"It's not that bad," so keep fighting (maybe). This sin? No big deal. Everyone does it, so don't worry so much about it. For example, "Everyone binges TV shows, who cares..." or "Everyone lives with someone before marriage. You have to see if you're sexually compatible first..." This perspective downplays the sin. But the reality is that all sin is rebellion against God. Eventually the fruit of this laziness is relinquishing the fight and making peace with this sin. But Jesus warns of the seriousness of sin in John 8:34, "Truly, truly, I say to you, everyone who practices sin is a slave to sin." Instead we must acknowledge this sin as the dangerous enemy that it is, and make war. Sin is a malignant cancer that left to itself will always grow and destroy.[14]

"Try harder!" And keep fighting. *More!* More strategy, more discipline, more accountability, more activity. For example, if someone is struggling with idolatry of food, they sign up for yet another dieting program, with an even stricter regimen. This might seem on the surface to be an invigorating response, but because it does not find power in the gospel it will be short-lived. It is an utterly exhausting treadmill. Paul warns against human teachings and reliance on human strength in Colossians 2:23, "These have indeed an appearance of wisdom in promoting self-made religion and asceticism and severity to the body, but they are of no value in stopping the indulgence of the flesh." The reality is that we have no power in ourselves to defeat our sin. Instead we must give up our self-help strategy and trust only in Jesus.

We must reject the counterfeits. We must remember the true gospel. This crucial first step humbles us before the Lord when we admit we have no power and need help. Paradoxically, this empowers us to have the energy and will to fight our sin. Step 2 of continuing the fight will naturally flow from Step 1 of remembering the gospel.

This Sin is Just the Tip of the Iceberg

Whatever your biggest struggle is right now, whether it is gluttony, money, video games, porn, academic idolatry, alcohol, or something else, it probably feels in some way like your *only* struggle. It's always on your mind, it's a primary topic in your discipleship and mentoring, and your feeling of spiritual maturity rises and falls based on your recent victories and failures in this arena. It's as if your entire spiritual life has been distilled down to this one topic. When you win, you're great! But when you lose, you tank.

Here's the discouraging reality: this besetting sin you're struggling with is not your *only* sin. It's probably not even your deepest and biggest sin. As the Spirit reveals more of your sin and convicts you of the presence of greater wickedness in your heart, you will begin to realize how you need the gospel in a deeper way. This is discouraging at first, but it bears good fruit in the end.

You're much worse than you think! But this is surprisingly good news. Jesus Christ did not come to earth to save you only from this *one* sin. He's not that small of a Rescuer! He's a whole-life Savior, and His goal for your growth and glory is so much bigger than you can imagine. He has initiated a complete life transformation. There was a time when I thought that porn was my biggest problem; I thought that was what God wanted to work on the most with me. But His plans were so much bigger: to transform my mind, my heart, my affections, my priorities, my character, my legacy, and my eternity. This is the amazing power of the gospel: it's not just a pragmatic strategy to give you victory over this one area of struggle. God wants your *whole* life to be transformed in holiness to bring maximum glory to Him.

So Why is God Allowing This?

So if God wants me to be holy, and this sin is offensive to him, and the Spirit is at work... then *why* is God allowing this? Especially since I want victory too, why isn't God helping me to win? If Christ died for this sin, and we both want it dead...why is this sin still alive? Why do I still struggle? What's the point? This was maddening to me in my struggle with porn. Why is the fight taking this long? I've prayed, I've asked God to help me, I'm doing everything I can to fight and win... why is God allowing this? Why isn't He answering my prayers? It feels like He has left me alone in the fight. I could resonate with Psalm 13:1, "How long, O Lord? Will you forget me forever? How long will you hide your face from me?"

This specific sin struggle is an arena where God can teach you *much*, and perhaps it may be the only way God can teach you these specific lessons, and drive your faith deeper in the gospel. Do you believe that God can use your evil for His good? This doesn't mean we keep on sinning so that grace increases (Romans 6:1). But we *do* trust the Lord in His timing. So press into the lessons that God is teaching you about the gospel: your sinfulness, and His provision in Christ. *Wait* for Him to bring the victory. God is greatly glorified by our dependence and trust in Him as we wait patiently. We show His worth as we struggle and strive to have Him alone be the recipient of our highest affections. The pain we feel as we repent and wait and suffer is the pain of worship. As we resist temptation and fight our old idols, we need to pray, "God, I will be satisfied by you, or I will remain unsatisfied. If patient pain is what you call me to, then so be it. You are worth it. I will worship you alone."

I was deeply ministered to by this wisdom from John Owen in his book *The Mortification of Sin*. It was published in 1656 so the English is challenging, please bear with me. He writes, "Do you think [God] will ease you of that which perplexes you, that you may be at liberty to that which no less grieves him? No. God says, 'Here is one, if he could be rid of this lust I should never hear of him more; let him wrestle with his, or he is lost'...How do you know but that God has suffered the lust wherewith you have been perplexed to get strength in you, and power over you, to chasten you for your other negligences and common lukewarmness in walking before him; at least to awaken you to the consideration of your ways, that you may make a thorough work and change in your course of walking with him?"[15] Or to put this in modern language: what if God is allowing this sin that you hate, in order to help you fight the other sins that He also hates? What if it is God's plan for you to fight *this* sin to train you to be a more disciplined warrior to fight *all* sin? Maybe this sin, and your frequent failure, forces you to read the Bible daily because you recognize your weakness and need. Maybe this sin struggle is hard enough that you finally admit to other Christians that you need help. Maybe this sin creates enough feelings of guilt and shame in you to finally break your pride and convince you beyond doubt that *you are a wicked sinner*, and therefore in need of God's grace and eligible for the gospel.[16] What if this struggle is God's gymnasium for you, strengthening you and equipping you strategically for *harder* fights in the future? What if our God is so wise and sovereign and gracious that He is able to use even our *failures* as a means of our further sanctification? We serve an amazing, patient, loving, wise God.

Therefore our fighting against deep sin should produce a deeper humility, a deeper fight against all our sin, a deeper repentance, and therefore a deeper dependence on the gospel and greater joy in Christ's salvation. It is a hard path, but the fruit is good in the end.

How Can You Remember the Gospel?

Hopefully you're convinced that you need to remember the gospel. But how do we do it? What are some practical, actionable, boots-on-the-ground ways to remember God's grace to us in Christ? We can't create faith in our hearts, we are dependent on God. And yet God has given us established methods and means. Let's look at three: we pray, read, and believe.

First, **pray**. You need God's help! Left to yourself, you will forget the gospel, and you'll go right back to whatever performance-based non-gospel you were functioning in before Christ. This is the sinful inclination of our hearts, to abandon Christ. Pray, *pray*, PRAY. Pray for God to remind you. Pray for God to stir your heart. Pray for the Holy Spirit to increase your affection for Jesus. Prayer is not a work we do to earn God's approval; prayer is not a substitute for the gospel. Rather, prayer is an outflow of our dependence on God. We cry out to Him for the help we need, the help that only He can give. One of the really helpful ways I've found to focus my prayers is by writing them out in a journal. It slows me down and helps me to concentrate.

Second, **read**. Read the Scriptures! Jesus gives this amazing promise in John 15:11, "These things I have spoken to you, that my joy may be in you, and that your joy may be full." Do you want joy? Joy in Jesus is the foundation of our fight against sin. When we are fully satisfied in Him, we have no more hunger for these failed substitute gods. It's a fight against counterfeit loves. If you want joy, then *read!* Read God's words. Pour the fertilizer of God's Word onto the wilting plant of your heart. Sprinkle the cool water of God's truths onto the dry and cracked ground of your mind. See life begin to come as the Spirit uses Scripture to restore your soul. Reading the Word is not a work we do to earn God's approval, but it is an act of faithful obedience. We respond to God's invitation to be spiritually filled with His food for our souls.

Third, **believe**. This is assumed, but let me make it explicit. You can't just pray and read and then sit back passively, waiting for God to do all the work. You must believe the gospel; this is part of God's work. Once you've read it or heard it or sung it... believe it! This takes effort. But wait... is this just another work we do? Is this another non-gospel? No, this is the same gospel. But believing in the gospel is a kind of work or effort, as Jesus says in John 6:29, "This is the work of God, that you believe in him whom he has sent." Or to give an example of the kind of "work" of believing, consider Psalm 42, as the writer counsels his own heart in v5-6, "Why are you cast down, O my soul, and why are you in turmoil within me? Hope in God; for I shall again praise him, my salvation and my

God. My soul is cast down within me; therefore I remember you from the land of Jordan and of Hermon, from Mount Mizar." The psalmist takes himself by the hand, asking questions, and setting his mind on trusting God. He makes effort to remember, and to believe in God. He works out his faith![17]

Practically, what are other ways to engage our hearts with this good news? The methods are endless: sing cross-centered songs, journal your prayers, memorize Scripture, ask other Christians to remind you of the gospel. You can put reminders on sticky notes or wallpapers on your smartphone screen, read theologically-rich books that stock your mind full of truths and explanations of the gospel, be regularly involved in a Bible-teaching church to hear the gospel being preached. You should seek out discipleship and counseling to help you discover your barriers so that you can push these truths deeper, find sermons online that will stir your heart for Jesus, and gather brothers and sisters in Christ that can remind you of the gospel when you forget. For me, I find that John Piper sermons really stir my affections for Jesus.[18]

But with all these things, it's not enough to simply hear the gospel, or read the gospel, or even intellectually comprehend the gospel. You have to *believe* it. That's part of remembering. It's the fight of faith. It's not solely a cerebral exercise; it's a remembering of the heart, a stirring of the affections towards Christ, and a setting of your trust and hope in Him *again*. Find what will remind you of Christ's love and rescue on the Cross. Discover what draws you back into intimacy with Him. Relentlessly fight to remember this good gospel.

The War is Won

In closing, consider the difference between the battles against sin and the larger war for the gospel. If you win a battle against sin, but lose the war for the gospel, you have accomplished a tactical victory but a strategic defeat. I'm not saying we should try to lose battles against sin. We should fight hard! But we have to get the focus and the order right. The focus is on the war for the gospel, not the battles against sin. This encourages us. And our task is to remember that the *war* is won in Christ, which empowers us to fight the battles. Because that ultimate war has been won, we can fight the remaining battles with confidence and hope that victory is certain. Christ has already *won!* This means we are always fighting a defeated enemy. That gives us great hope.

Christian, remember the gospel.

INTERMISSION: THE PIVOT

"When rightly understood, God's love will propel you toward holiness and growth in grace. The order is essential: I am a new creation, accepted, adopted, and free; therefore I want to please God. We do not say: I will try to please God so that I may become a new creation, make myself acceptable, and hope that God adopts me and sets me free." – Timothy Lane and Paul David Tripp, How People Change[19]

****

The gospel is amazing! I hope you are encouraged as you finished the last two chapters. But here in the intermission we must ask the pivot question: how does the truth of the gospel motivate and empower us to fight our sin? How does Step 1 (Remember the gospel) lead us to Step 2 (Keep fighting)? Is it possible to remember the gospel...and not fight our sin? We can put the answer in theological terms: justification leads to sanctification. Being one *with* Christ leads to becoming more *like* Christ. Forgiveness of sin motivates fighting of sin. Jesus kills our sin on the cross, so we kill the sin in our lives. We are declared righteous, therefore we develop in righteousness. Paul reasons in Romans 6 that our union with Christ calls us to consider ourselves dead to sin, and now slaves of righteousness. We cannot remain in our sin!

English grammar terms can help us understand this theological concept: **the indicative drives the**

imperative. The *indicative* is a statement of being, "The chair is green." The *imperative* is a statement of command, "Paint the chair green." And the distinction between these two grammatical concepts is one of the most glorious and empowering truths of Christianity. In regular life, you have to *do* something before you *are* something. You have to practice hours every day to become a Broadway violin player. You have to weightlift for months before you can become a chiseled athlete. But in the Bible, the indicative comes first, *then* the imperative. This is so counter-cultural, and powerful! What this means is that *who* you are comes before *what* you should do. "I *am* saved by Christ." And therefore, *"Kill* sin." The order is *being*, then *doing*. It is first *identity*, then *activity*. It's actually a false gospel to put the order the other way around! We don't deserve our adoption, it is by grace. We don't perform righteous acts in order to earn our righteousness, Christ earns it and gives it. "Imperative before indicative" is the counterfeit of the gospel, it is merely man-made religion. Paul warns us in Galatians 2:21, "I do not nullify the grace of God, for if righteousness were through the law, then Christ died for no purpose." We can't earn it, we must receive it.

Where do we see the indicative drive the imperative? Let's examine this more deeply in God's Word:

- ❖ 1 John 3:1-3, "See what great love the Father has lavished on us, that we should be called children of God! And that is what we are! The reason the world does not know us is that it did not know him. Dear friends, now we are children of God, and what we will be has not yet been made known. But we know that when Christ appears, we shall be like him, for we shall see him as he is. All who have this hope in him purify themselves, just as he is pure." We are loved children (indicative); and so we purify ourselves (imperative).

❖ Ephesians 4:1, "As a prisoner for the Lord, then, I urge you to live a life worthy of the calling you have received." You have received a calling (indicative); now live a life worthy of it (imperative).

❖ Colossians 3:1-5, "Since, then, you have been raised with Christ, set your hearts on things above, where Christ is, seated at the right hand of God. Set your minds on things above, not on earthly things. For you died, and your life is now hidden with Christ in God. When Christ, who is your life, appears, then you also will appear with him in glory. Put to death, therefore, whatever belongs to your earthly nature..." You have been raised with Christ and your life is now hidden with Him (indicative); so then set your hearts on things above and put to death what is earthly (imperative).

❖ Galatians 5:24-25, "Those who belong to Christ Jesus have crucified the flesh with its passions and desires. Since we live by the Spirit, let us keep in step with the Spirit." Those in Christ have their old life crucified and now live by the Spirit (indicative); therefore forsake the flesh and keep in step with the Spirit (imperative).

❖ 1 Corinthians 5:7-8, "Get rid of the old yeast, so that you may be a new unleavened batch—as you really are. For Christ, our Passover lamb, has been sacrificed. Let us therefore celebrate the festival, not with the old leaven, the leaven of malice and evil, but with the unleavened bread of sincerity and truth." Amazing! This is one of the most clear of all the Scriptures. We're presented first with the *imperative*: get rid of the old yeast! But it's backed up by the *indicative*: you really are a new batch! Paul is essentially saying, *"Be who you are."* Christ our Passover lamb has been sacrificed in our place. That is what makes us new.

By grace we are *forgiven* of sin, and then told to start living *free* of sin. God rescued Israel by grace out of the slavery of Egypt, and *then* gave them the Law at Sinai. So this means we live a paradoxical Christian life. Martin Luther described this in Latin, *"simul justus et peccator"* which translates to "simultaneously just and sinner."[20] This means we are healed and healing, fixed and being worked on, justified and being sanctified, cleaned and getting cleaned up, unleavened and cleaning out the old leaven, Spirit-filled and yet with indwelling sin in our flesh (Romans 7), pure but still striving for purity. Our justification empowers our sanctification. Christ has made us new creations, therefore we live new lives.

When we remember the gospel, it empowers us to keep fighting our sin. And that fight is the focus of our next two chapters.

CHAPTER 5: KEEP FIGHTING (DEFEND)

"If, then, sin will be always acting, if we be not always mortifying, we are lost creatures. He that stands still and suffers his enemies to double blows upon him without resistance will undoubtedly be conquered in the issue. If sin be subtle, watchful, strong, and always at work in the business of killing our souls, and we be slothful, negligent, foolish, in proceeding to the ruin thereof, can we expect a comfortable event? There is not a day but sin foils or is foiled, prevails or is prevailed on; and it will be so while we live in this world. ...The saints, whose souls breathe after deliverance from its [i.e., sin's] perplexing rebellion, know there is no safety against it but in a constant warfare." – John Owen, *The Mortification of Sin*[21]

****

When you remember the gospel, you are motivated to keep fighting your sin. This is good and right. If Christ has died for this sin, how then can I live in it any longer? If Christ has set me free from this sin, how then can I still live as a slave? But let's get practical; I want to give you the best equipment for the fight. You need weapons for battle, you need equipment for combat.

Ephesians 4:22-24 calls us "to put off your old self, which belongs to your former manner of life and is corrupt through deceitful desires, and to be renewed in the spirit of your minds, and to put on the new self, created after the likeness of God in true righteousness and holiness." There's a double command of *put off* and *put on*: the fight against sin is both defensive and offensive. We stop old things, and we start new things. Theologians call this mortification (killing of sin) and vivification (spiritual growth). Both are necessary to make progress in sanctification.

The next two chapters focus on six key strategies to fight our sin. In chapter 5, three are defensive: Stronger Together, The Battlefield, and Use Your Sword. In chapter 6, the next three are offensive: Get to the Heart, The Counter-Attack, and Join the Mission. In all of these, you'll need to contextualize these strategies to your own situation. Everybody is different in the nuances of his or her fight, so you'll need to develop a custom battle plan and figure out what works best. Also, you'll benefit most from these strategies by processing through them with other Christians, perhaps your pastor or mentor or roommate. They can help you see how to specifically apply these principles into the context of *your* fight.

And most importantly: do *not* skip Step 1, "remember the gospel." If you skip the gospel, you will have no power to endure in the fight. You'll be running into battle naked and unarmed. John Owen writes in his book *The Mortification of Sin* about the stupidity of fighting sin without the gospel and help of the Holy Spirit, "Mortification from a self-strength, carried on by ways of self-invention, unto the end of a self-righteousness, is the soul and substance of all false religion in the world."[22] We must trust in Christ, not ourselves! Again Owen writes, "Mortification of any sin must be by a supply of grace. Of ourselves we cannot do it."[23] All of the six strategies discussed in these chapters are a component of Step 2, "keep fighting." This fighting is powerful and effective and necessary, but "keep fighting" is still humbly Step 2. We must *first* remember the gospel, and *then* keep fighting. The order is crucial.

I pray that God radically empowers you to use these six strategies to wage massive war against your sins and to make diligent progress in your sanctification. But before we begin, let's clarify what repentance is.

What is Repentance?

Repentance in its most basic definition is *change*. Change of mind, change of heart, and change of behavior. Repentance is not merely remembering the gospel on an intellectual level. It's also changing and doing things differently. So repentance means a life-transforming activity that can be witnessed by others. And this is motivated by the gospel.

Repentance is also relational: we change because we know God is grieved by our sin. We know that our intimacy with Him is interrupted by our rebellion. We long for relationship with Him again. It is God's love for us that prompts our response of love back to Him. This love motivates our life change. It's like a husband seeing how his unkind words hurt his wife. Because she loves him and he loves her, he changes. Romans 2:4 indicates that God's kindness leads us to repentance.

The first of the 95 theses of Martin Luther was, "When our Lord and Master, Jesus Christ, said 'Repent,' He called for the entire life of believers to be one of repentance."[24] Repentance is the chief characteristic of the Christian; it is the key to long-term growth and change. It's the core of our spiritual life, Ben Stuart describes our sanctification as "one movement with two parts," mortification and vivification.[25] To grow spiritually we must kill sin and cultivate holiness. We must turn away from sin and turn towards Christ. In Mark 1:15 when Jesus began His ministry He preached, "The time is fulfilled, and the kingdom of God is at hand; repent and believe in the gospel." So we see that repentance and gospel go hand in hand. After we have remembered the gospel, we are motivated to fight our sin. The gospel-powered fight produces life change; this is all part of the process of repentance.

When should you repent? Right now. Continually. Immediately. Anytime you feel conviction by the Holy Spirit, you should respond in repentance. And this is done repeatedly throughout the Christian life. May these six strategies help you to "bear fruit in keeping with repentance" (Matthew 3:8). Let's begin by strengthening your defense against sin.

1. Stronger Together: Fighting in Community

The fight is hard. But you don't have to fight alone. God has built up the body of Christ around you, to fight *with* you. To strengthen you. To rush into combat alongside you. To help you win.

James 5:16 states it so clearly, "Therefore, confess your sins to one another and pray for one another, that you may be healed." Galatians 6:1-2 further exhorts us to fight sin with the power of community, "Brothers, if anyone is caught in any transgression, you who are spiritual should restore him in a spirit of gentleness. Keep watch on yourself, lest you too be tempted. Bear one another's burdens, and so fulfill the law of Christ." Ecclesiastes 4:9-12 gives us a very practical argument for accountability, "Two are better than one, because they have a good reward for their toil. For if they fall, one will lift up his fellow. But woe to him who is alone when he falls and has not another to lift him up! Again, if two lie together, they keep warm, but how can one keep warm alone? And though a man might prevail against one who is alone, two will withstand him—a threefold cord is not quickly broken."

How do we live out these Scriptures? Here are four practical applications:

Pursue Community: Get involved in a deep community of folks who together are pursuing holiness and maturity in Christ. This is the vision of the local church. If you don't have this, *get this*. Find it. Create it if you have to. You may have to be intentional—even pioneering—and cultivate this community. Share with a sister about your struggle with cutting. Share with a brother about your struggle with porn.[26] Explain to your community group how you're struggling with anger. Call an older woman and talk about your fight with food. Reach out and come into the light (1 John 1:9), there is such freedom in being open! Likewise there is real danger in being a solitary Christian, so don't go it alone or you'll be an easy target. And don't seek out brothers and sisters only once in some big display of repentance, but seek out Christians *often*, maybe even *daily*, as you fight temptation and face failure. Consider joining an online or in-person support group.[27]

Practice Radical Confession: What happens when you fail? James 5:16 says we should confess our sins to one another and *pray* for each other so that we can be healed.

Confession is not done only to God, but also to our sisters and brothers. Our sin is made known! Sin thrives in secret, but if we drag it out into the light it loses its power. Confess your sin! Betray it, don't protect it any more in the darkness. Richard Baxter writes in his *Christian Directory*, "If less means prevail not, open thy case to some able, faithful friend, and engage them to watch over thee; and tell them when thou art most endangered by the temptation. This will shame thee from the sin, and lay more engagements on thee to forbear it... Concealment is Satan's great advantage. It would be hard for thee to sin thus if it were but opened."[28]

Submit to Accountability: Confess, and then get accountability. Have people follow up with you about it, ask them to pray for you every week. Share with them your battlefield of when and where you're most tempted. Ask them to ask *you* about it. Tell them that they have permanent free access to bring up this topic with you every week. Consider also submitting to discipline as part of accountability. You don't want your "accountability" to be merely a cathartic evacuation of guilt without any real lasting change. Establish an agreement with your friends or spouse or church leadership about the consequences you'll face if you have a sinful failure. This is not punishment (that has been taken by Christ) but is meant to help you see and experience the pain and consequences that come with your sin. Paul Worcester shares this example, "I told my Dad that each time I gave into temptation I would give our Church $100! Guess how many times I gave in? Twice! I paid my $200 and then went a very long time until I struggled with it again. That is what it took for me to motivate myself to overcome my addiction."[29] Real, painful consequences can provide an extra boost for awareness of sin and motivation to fight. But beware the subtle temptation of your primary motivation becoming "avoidance of consequences" instead of the glorious gospel.

Help Others: You are not the only one struggling! Open your eyes to the hurting people around you. They are in the trenches of sin, fighting with all the strength they can, but they're discouraged and tired and lonely *just like you*. Reach out to them, ask them how they're doing, and *pray* with them. Give them the help you wish you had! You will be surprised how encouraging it is to *you* and how much new strength comes into *your* fight as you pour out into others to help them in *their* fight. Text someone, grab a lunch, make a phone call, or check in at church. These are your brothers and sisters; they desire encouragement and accountability too. You need them, and they need you.

Here's an example of "stronger together" in my life: I had a small handful of faithful brothers that I would text when I felt tempted, when I had failed, when I was struggling with guilt, when I needed encouragement. And I had an even larger group of 25 brothers that I would email periodically with an update on the fight. I broadened the circle of help as wide as I could, to get as much help as I could. Don't wait for people to contact you; *you* take initiative to create the community of help that you need. If you fight alone, you will lose alone.

This is war. You cannot do it by yourself; the enemy is too strong, and you have blind spots. You are weak by yourself, but mighty in community. God has given you brothers and sisters, you can fight stronger together! You are not alone in the trenches; you have fellow soldiers who are going through the same temptations and struggles. Open your eyes and call out for help! There is strength in numbers.

2. The Battlefield: Where/When/How

The fight doesn't happen in a vacuum. The fight happens on the battlefield. There is a location, a time, and a way you're being attacked. What is your battlefield? Once you can discern your battlefield, you can create a tactical map of your temptation, so you can fight with wisdom.

Romans 13:14 is one of the most helpful passages in the entire Bible as a strategy for fighting our sin. Paul writes, "But put on the Lord Jesus Christ, and make no provision for the flesh, to gratify its desires." This leads us to ask this crucial question: "How are you making provision for the flesh?" Or to put it in business terms: "What is the supply chain for your sin?" Pray for God to give you insight and understanding.

Let's get practical by asking some questions:

Where are you tempted? What location? Do you notice any patterns? Maybe your dorm room? A certain store? At the gym? The bathroom, the beach, your parent's home? Where you're alone? Or where you're with people? For many college students, heading to their parent's home over Thanksgiving break, Christmas break, or especially over the summer can be a time of increased temptation and spiritual dryness.

When are you tempted? When during the day? Afternoon? After 10pm? What's the situation? Is it a certain day of the week? Early morning? Certain seasons of the year? After work or after putting the kids to bed or after finals week is over? What is unique about that time of the day that makes it challenging or discouraging? What's your emotional state during that part of the week?

How are you tempted? How are you getting access to the sin? If your struggle is with food, is it items in your pantry, your fridge, church snacks, or restaurants where you go out to eat? If it's comparison or jealousy, is it through social media that you are viewing the glamourous lives of others you envy? If it's porn, what device are you using to get on the internet? If it's sloth and worshipping entertainment, is it TV shows, movies, or video games? If it's greed and materialism, is it online shopping, advertisements, and Black Friday deals? What are the tools that are resourcing your sin? Who is your supplier? What's the method?

Once we are able to answer these questions, we can accurately identify our battlefield. Now we can use this knowledge to craft a battle plan. Get creative! How can you cut off the supply chain? How can you interrupt this battlefield? What locations can you avoid? What times of day do you need increased accountability and prayer? What websites should you block? What old friends do you need to stop spending time with? What apps do you need to delete? Pray for God to give you sanctified creativity and lead you towards specific applications. Make a battle plan! But don't put your trust in your plan, instead "put on the Lord Jesus Christ" first and then as a step 2, make a plan.

Let me share several examples from my life. When I was struggling with playing too many video games, I took my power cord out of the console and stored it in my sock drawer. This created a road bump and interrupted my habit of getting home and mindlessly turning on the games. When I was struggling deeply with porn, I used to take my laptop and phone out to my car for the night, and store them there while I went back inside to go to sleep. When I struggle with focusing on my phone and ignoring my family, I put my phone in a cupboard so I'm not tempted to pull it out and start scrolling. When I struggle with mindlessly eating junk food, my wife has suggested that I control my portion size by putting some chips in a bowl instead of sitting on the couch with the whole bag. It is *so* helpful having the access taken away! The fight becomes easier.

Know your battlefield, and create a battle plan.

3. Use Your Sword: Wield the Word of God

In Ephesians 6:10-20, Paul exhorts us to put on the whole armor of God. He lists many pieces of equipment: shield, breastplate, and helmet. The Word of God is described as our sword, and we must learn how to wield it powerfully. So many Christians seem to *know* Scriptures, but they aren't *using* them. You have a Sword! Use it! Swing it, slice against the lies, chop down the counterfeits, and hack away at the seductions. God has not sent you off into battle naked and unequipped. Don't sit there getting attacked and tempted, and thinking you can't do anything about it. Use your sword! You must learn to wield the Word of God to defend yourself against sin.

When Jesus was tempted by Satan in the wilderness, He responded to each of Satan's offers by quoting Scripture (Matthew 4:1-11). That was Jesus' tactic. He used the Word of God to combat lies and stand strong against evil. Three times Satan comes at Jesus with temptations. And three times Jesus says, "It is written" (Matthew 4:4, 7, 10) and quotes specific Scripture that counteracts the lies He just heard. Eventually Satan admits defeat and leaves Him alone.

When the late pastor E.V. Hill preached on Matthew 4 at Promise Keepers in 1993, he emphasized this very point: Jesus responded to temptation with Scripture. Hill exhorted those men in application, "Hit that devil with the Word... Hit 'em! Hit 'em!"[30] You have to learn some good punches! You have to know truths from God's Word that can be used to combat the lies.

There are two parts to this strategy:

1. What temptation? Figure out what your specific temptation is. It's not always clear, so think about it and write it down. Maybe ask a friend to help you see what it is. What is your sin promising? What are you being invited to do? What's the allure?

2. What Scripture? Research what specific Scripture speaks to that temptation. Think about it. Write those Scripture passages down. Memorize them. What does God promise? How is Jesus more appealing? What Scripture counteracts this temptation?

Let's consider some temptations, and what Scripture might be used in defense:

Ricardo's Temptation: "You'll be accepted by others if you have cool clothing." Scripture: Romans 14:18, "Whoever thus serves Christ is acceptable to God and approved by men." 2 Corinthians 10:18, "For it is not the one who commends himself who is approved, but the one whom the Lord commends."

Kathleen's Temptation: "Eating this chocolate cake will make you happy." Scripture: Psalm 16:11, "You make known to me the path of life. In your presence there is fullness of joy; at your right hand are pleasures forevermore." Hebrews 13:9, "Do not be led away by diverse and strange teachings, for it is good for the heart to be strengthened by grace, not by foods, which have not benefited those devoted to them."

Christina's Temptation: "Porn will give you rest and comfort." Scripture: 1 Corinthians 6:18, "Flee from sexual immorality. Every other sin a person commits is outside the body, but the sexually immoral person sins against his own body." Matthew 11:28-30, "Come to me, all who labor and are heavy laden, and I will give you rest. Take my yoke upon you, and learn from me, for I am gentle and lowly in heart, and you will find rest for your souls. For my yoke is easy, and my burden is light."

Monique's Temptation: "Share your idea right now with this person because your idea is better and they need to hear it." Scripture: James 1:19, "Know this, my beloved brothers: let every person be quick to hear, slow to speak, slow to anger..." Philippians 2:3, "Do nothing from selfish ambition or conceit, but in humility count others more significant than yourselves."

Jonathan's Temptation: "Video games will be more exciting than reading the Bible." Scripture: 2 Timothy 3:16-17, "All Scripture is breathed out by God and profitable for teaching, for reproof, for correction, and for training in righteousness, that the man of God may be complete, equipped for every good work." Hebrews 11:6, "And without faith it is impossible to please him, for whoever would draw near to God must believe that he exists and that he rewards those who seek him."

A number of years ago, I committed Proverbs 5:15-23 to memory, and recited it often as I faced sexual temptation. Being a longer passage, it helped to deliberately center my mind on truth. In my struggle with overwork and the idolatry of productivity, I've memorized Romans 4:4-5, "Now to the one who works, his wages are not counted as a gift but as his due. And to the one who does not work but believes in him who justifies the ungodly, his faith is counted as righteousness..." Get the Scripture in your mind, so you can use it to fight. Psalm 119:11 says, "I have stored up your word in my heart, that I might not sin against you." Sadly the discipline of Scripture memory in our day has often been downplayed. But Jesus gives us a challenging example. He quotes three times from Deuteronomy! How many of us can quote Old Testament Law to counteract temptation? But remember the effect: when Jesus quotes Scripture, Satan leaves Jesus. In the face of the Word, Satan admits defeat.

Defend yourself with the Bible. Christian, pick up your sword.

CHAPTER 6: KEEP FIGHTING (ATTACK)

"Part of sin is dissatisfaction with God. Lust's power comes from the promise it gives that something besides God can make us happy. What this means is that the only way to overcome the power of lust in our lives is by finding better promises. The key to holiness is satisfaction in God—faith that He is more to be desired than anything this world has to offer. We're not just turning away from lust; we're turning toward true satisfaction and joy in God."
– Joshua Harris, Sex is Not the Problem (Lust Is)[31]

****

As we face the onslaught of sin and temptation, we must respond with a powerful defense. We need the strength of community, the wisdom of battlefield tactics, and the hammer of God's Word. But we can't stop at merely defense. God calls us to get down deep to the heart level, to find our satisfaction and joy in Him, and to join His mission of rescue in our hurting world. We must respond with a powerful attack. The next three offensive strategies are: Get to the Heart, The Counter-Attack, and Join the Mission.

4. Get to the Heart: Discover the Base

In real-time strategy (RTS) video games, there's always a home base. From that base and other buildings, you generate fighting units. If you're battling an enemy and all you do is attack the fighting units, you will never win. You must find their hidden command center, and attack the base. You must destroy the buildings that create the fighting units. If you don't, it's like mopping up water but not turning off the faucet. It'll never work!

In the fight against our sin, we need to go deeper. We need to not only hack off the fruit; we need to figure out what is at the root. In biblical language, we need to move past the behavior and get to the heart. In Scripture the idea of the heart is rich and multifaceted; the heart is the seat of our affections, our desires, and our motivations. We think with our heart as it governs our life, and we believe with our heart, as it drives our behavior. Jesus says in Mark 7:20-23, "What comes out of a person is what defiles him. For from within, out of the heart of man, come evil thoughts, sexual immorality, theft, murder, adultery, coveting, wickedness, deceit, sensuality, envy, slander, pride, foolishness. All these evil things come from within, and they defile a person."

To truly make progress in our fight against sin, we need to ask this crucial question: *Why* do you turn to this sin? What are you believing? What is this sin offering? This is the *why* of the Battlefield. What is motivating you to run to this sin? Are you feeling lonely, angry, hungry, tired, discouraged? Are you feeling like you've worked hard and now you deserve a break? Do you feel like God has cheated you and this is your way of getting what you *need*? Why are you running after *this* particular sin? What is it offering you? Pleasure? Acceptance? Identity?[32]

First, as you recognize the "why", you can replace it with the superior promises of God. What He offers is better! Jeremiah 2:12-13 says, "Be appalled, O heavens, at this; be shocked, be utterly desolate, declares the LORD, for my people have committed two evils: they have forsaken me, the fountain of living waters, and hewed out cisterns for themselves, broken cisterns that can hold no water." Do you see how God is better? He is the fountain of living waters. We thirst, and only He provides. When we go to our sin, it is tragically a broken cistern. It fails to deliver the satisfaction it promises.

Second, as we recognize the depth of our hearts, we must repent even deeper. You're not simply repenting of the sinful *action*. You need to realize that those actions are coming from your *heart*. At the deepest level you have forsaken God. You need not merely behavior change; you need *heart* change, which means you need the power of the gospel.

Here are a few examples of what this deeper heart focus looks like:

Ricardo is spending significant money on new technology and designer clothing. Behavior-change would give him tips on stewardship and help him form a budget. But heart change goes to the impulse: he loves the praise of man; he believes that he'll be accepted if he has the latest gear.

Kathleen continues to overeat. Behavior-change would advise a strict diet, a mobile app to track calories, maybe even a group of supporters to encourage her progress. But heart change goes much deeper: she goes to food to find comfort. That slice of chocolate cake is promising anesthesia to the pain in her life; she believes that food gives what God can't.

Christina is struggling with looking at pornography. Behavior-change would advise an internet filter or switching to a dumbphone. But heart change goes to the reason: she's lonely and angry at God for not providing a husband. Looking at porn is her way of coping; she believes porn will give the comfort that God won't.

Monique talks excessively, often talking over others. Behavior-change would recommend learning some good listening techniques. But heart change goes to the root: she is prideful and selfish; she believes that what she has to say is more important than what everyone else has to say.

Jonathan can't seem to get consistent time reading the Bible. Behavior-change would recommend a reading plan, an alarm clock, and a self-help video on time management. But heart change goes to the affections: Jonathan does not value the Word of God, and has little hunger to hear from God; he believes academics and video games are more entertaining and important.

Focusing on the heart shows our deeper need for the gospel. We don't just need tactics and todos that change our behavior, we need to get to the root and experience change from the inside out. But how can we do this? We need a Savior who will give us a new heart, and we need the Holy Spirit to transform and renew our minds. We need the gospel! And the good news is that the gospel doesn't merely give us new behavior, it first gives us new hearts with new affections and loves and goals.

True and lasting change comes from the heart. So we must get down to the heart level to understand our motivations and desires. It was helpful for me to begin exploring the reasons I was turning to porn for comfort: I was tired, I was anxious, I was overwhelmed, I was lonely.

There were powerful heart-level motivations that drove me to this idol. But those same motivations could drive me instead to Jesus, and be satisfied in Him! What are those drives for you? What are you feeling and believing? Pray! Call out to God to change your heart, ask Him to switch your affections, and plead with Him to give you satisfaction in Jesus as the fountain of living waters. He is better. When we are satisfied in Jesus at the heart level, then our behavior changes drastically. How can we cultivate this new affection for Jesus? That's what our next strategy is all about.

5. The Counter-Attack: Joy in Jesus

D-Day is one of the most well-known invasions in history. Allied forces landed in the beaches of Normandy to take back Europe from Nazi Germany. Think with me for a moment: what if Allied forces decided to only defend? They might have said, "Well, France is lost, but let's just hold the channel. We'll make sure they don't progress into England." Would this be victory? No! Military commanders understood that a counter-attack was necessary. They needed to go on the offensive.

The same is true in the fight against sin. Don't fight only defensively; you must also fight offensively! Some Christians are really good at defense: they have strategies for *when* temptation comes, they have strategies to try to avoid the battles, and they have sisters or brothers to confess to after they fail. But because they're not fighting offensively, they're not actually making progress in the fight. If you fight only defensively, the best scenario is a standstill. That's not progress. The Scriptures call us to put off *and* to put on, to fight against sin *and* pursue holiness.

What does it mean to fight offensively? What is the counter-attack? The answer is cultivating a superior affection for Christ. You will never change unless you love Jesus *more* than you love sin. Our aim is that Jesus becomes more beautiful to us than the allure of our sin. And when we are deeply and fully satisfied in Him, we won't have hunger for our sin anymore! We will be full. Proverbs 27:7 says it well, "One who is full loathes honey, but to one who is hungry everything bitter is sweet." Consider: who wants to eat a stale granola bar when they just finished a meal an all-you-can-eat buffet? Who wants to watch a dumb cat video at the top of Mount Everest? Who would pull out their phone to check the latest celebrity gossip on social media at their own wedding reception? See, when we are satisfied with great pleasures, we aren't tempted by small trifles. **The goal is to glut yourself on Christ so you're always satisfied.** Not only does this protect us from the allure of sin, but it provides us the deepest joys and gives God the most glory. It's a fabulous win/win! John Piper has famously said, "God is most glorified in us when we are most satisfied in Him."[33]

Consider how Scriptures speaks of the superior joy found in Jesus:

- ❖ Psalm 16:11, "You make known to me the path of life; in your presence there is fullness of joy; at your right hand are pleasures forevermore."
- ❖ Psalm 84:10, "For a day in your courts is better than a thousand elsewhere. I would rather be a

doorkeeper in the house of my God than dwell in the tents of wickedness."

❖ Psalm 73:25-26, "Whom have I in heaven but you? And there is nothing on earth that I desire besides you. My flesh and my heart may fail, but God is the strength of my heart and my portion forever."

Jesus is *better!* What He offers is greater. His joy is full, His pleasure is superior, His comfort is top-shelf, His presence is all-satisfying. Why would you turn away from this glorious Savior to pursue lesser lovers?

So how can you cultivate greater affection for Jesus? We must present to our minds and hearts the beauty of Jesus, seen most clearly in the gospel of our redemption. Consider these practical applications that will stir your joy in Jesus:

Read the Bible: This is where we see Jesus most clearly! God has given us 66 books in His library of communication to us. And every one of these books is about Jesus (Luke 24:27). Commit to a consistent time, a place, and a reading plan.[34] Do whatever it takes to get that Scripture in you: read quickly and slowly, read broadly and deeply. Consume large quantities of Scripture; or carefully pick through a passage in study. Search out truth that will make your heart sing. Memorize, meditate, and enjoy. Jesus makes this offer in John 15:11, "These things I have spoken to you, that my joy may be in you, and that your joy may be full."

Sing: When we are really happy, we sing! But song also helps to set our hearts on an object of joy. Worship corporately with large groups of other Christians.

Worship in small groups. Worship by yourself. Saturate your mind and heart with songs of His grace. Seek out songs that are soaked in Scripture. Find the songs that stir your affections. Gather the songs that exalt Jesus and remind you of the gospel. Here are some of my favorite songs: "Jesus My Only Hope," "He Will Hold Me Fast," "Before the Throne of God Above," "O for a Thousand Tongues to Sing," and "Jesus is Better."

Pray: How are you going to grow in affection for Christ if you aren't talking with Him every day? Do people fall in love by ignoring each other? Speak with Him. Share your thoughts, fears, dreams, and ideas. Ask Him for help, for comfort, for encouragement, for forgiveness. Speak back to Jesus about His perfections, His glory, and His character. Express your gratitude for His salvation. Pray for others in their struggles. Pray relentlessly.[35]

Read Solid Christian books: Learn satisfying truths about Jesus through solid books by authors who know and believe God's Word. Read about Jesus, read about the gospel, read about His kingdom, and read about His mission. Feed your mind! Nourish your soul with weighty truth. You were made to be satisfied with the greatness of God, so if you are starving your soul and feeding it trivialities, you will shrivel up. John Piper once recommended to a 17-year old man that he read all 1,200 pages of *Systematic Theology* by Wayne Grudem as one method of fighting lust.[36] Check out Appendix C for a list of book recommendations.

Love the Local Church: Be deeply involved in a local community of believers who will help you to apply these strategies, pray for you, and keep you accountable if you slack. A local church also provides biblical preaching and training to stock your mind full of truth from God's Word. Be convicted, challenged, and encouraged by passionate sermons about Jesus. If you're not involved in a church, do you really think you can go it alone? If you're not hearing God's Word preached, what *are* you hearing preached? God has blessed you with adoption into His family; avail yourself of this mighty resource to fight your sin.

And keep at it! Don't be discouraged if you aren't feeling deeply satisfied right away. Cultivating affection for Christ is similar to exercise. It takes some time to see the results. Endure. This is worth it. Keep pressing in to Jesus and keep patiently waiting for Him to bring the joy. I can't tell you how many mornings I have opened up my Bible, hoping that God would bring satisfaction to my soul, only to feel like it was just black words on a white page. I often feel spiritually thirsty and dry, and not nearly as happy in Jesus as I want to be. What do we do when we feel this? We cannot change our own hearts, but we are called to make use of the means of grace that God has identified. Sometimes we simply must force feed ourselves the Word of God,[37] lest we starve spiritually. He has given us tools to cultivate our affections, to set Jesus before the eyes of our soul. Use the means of grace! Remember this exhortation and encouragement from Philippians 2:12-13, "Therefore, my beloved, as you have always obeyed, so now, not only as in my presence but much more in my absence, work out your own salvation with fear and trembling, for it is God who works in you, both to will and to work for his good pleasure." We work, because God works in us.

6. Join the Mission: Fight for Jesus

What is your mission? What is your life purpose? Why are you here on this earth? What motivates you, drives you, and gets you out of bed in the morning? Without a driving purpose, we lose our energy and momentum, and become so quickly distracted by lesser things. We were made to be wrapped up in glorious purpose, to live lives filled with meaning, and to give ourselves fully to something *bigger* than us.

Jesus has invited the church to join His mission to make disciples of all nations. Read what He says in Matthew 28:18-20, "All authority in heaven and on earth has been given to me. Go therefore and make disciples of all nations, baptizing them in the name of the Father and of the Son and of the Holy Spirit, teaching them to observe all that I have commanded you. And behold, I am with you always, to the end of the age."

Isn't this exciting? The God of the Universe, who has *all* authority, has invited *you* to join Him in the mission that He is accomplishing globally. This is an unimaginable privilege! This is the job offer of a lifetime. He could do His mission all by Himself, but He has chosen to involve us—redeemed sinners—to be His hands and feet and mouth. Paul writes in 2 Corinthians 5:18-20, "All this is from God, who through Christ reconciled us to himself and gave us the ministry of reconciliation; that is, in Christ God was reconciling the world to himself, not counting their trespasses against them, and entrusting to us the message of reconciliation. Therefore, we are ambassadors for Christ, God making his appeal through us. We implore you on behalf of Christ, be reconciled to God." We have been reconciled to God and appointed as His ambassadors, commissioned to represent Him and reconcile the world! Amazing.

There is so much work to be done in our world. As of 2019, mission agencies estimate there are 3 billion unreached people groups, located mostly in the 10/40 window: 10 degrees north of the equator to 40 degrees encompassing West Africa, the Middle East, and Asia. Unreached means "a people group among which there is no indigenous community of believing Christians with adequate numbers and resources to evangelize this people group without outside assistance"[38] They won't know Jesus unless someone crosses cultural, geographic, and linguistic barriers to preach to them. Let's go, let's go! Join the mission by praying, giving, sending, and even going. Move outward in love towards the lost in the world. Share your joy in Jesus with others; this will increase your joy.

Christ calls us to preach the gospel, make disciples, and mobilize missionaries. This is part of why you need to fight your sin, so that you can be effective at His mission! When you're busy on mission, it takes time and energy. And it's exciting! You will find that you don't have as much time or energy to give to TV shows, shopping, video games, social media, and other distractions because your time is filled up with preaching the gospel, making disciples, serving others, and building up the church. The pursuit of the mission takes precedence over the pursuit of comfort; and doing what we were called and created to do gives great satisfaction.

Joining Jesus' mission might be what God uses as a catalyst to help you defeat your sin. Consider what David Mathis writes in *Habits of Grace*, "We will only go so deep with Jesus until we start yearning to reach out. When our life in him is healthy and vibrant, we not only ache to keep sinking our roots down deep in him, but we also want to stretch out our branches and extend his goodness to others. But not only does going deep with Jesus soon lead us to reach out to others, but also reaching out leads us deeper with him. In other words, getting on board with Jesus's mission to disciple the nations may be the very thing he uses to push through your spiritual lethargy and jump-start your stalled sanctification."[39] Get busy!

Jesus is the Captain of a rescue ship, not a cruise ship. If you're on board His ship, you can expect to be helping Him with the rescue effort! We have a wild-eyed Captain who is constantly throwing life preservers overboard, and calling us to do likewise. How can you sit on the deck and ask where your margarita is, when there are so many people suffering and drowning in the water right below? How can you be so focused on your comfort, especially when you *know* the means to rescue them? You too were rescued from that very same water; it was Christ who rescued you! Far too many Christians think of Christianity as a cruise ship, and they look tragically silly as consumers and complainers while the world is dying.

How do you start today? Begin by praying, then making a disciple right where you are. A disciple is a committed follower of Jesus, a person who believes and lives like Jesus is their Savior, Lord, and Treasure. Are you a mother? Make disciples of your children. Are you a professional? Invite a coworker to lunch to share the gospel with them. Are you a church member? Choose a younger person in your church and meet with them weekly to help them grow in their faith. Are you a student? Grab a new student and read the Bible together at the cafeteria, and ask them to invite their non-Christian friends to join. Pray that God blesses your efforts, and then take a bold step of faith with the opportunities right in front of you. As you step forward and join in Jesus' mission, I promise there is great joy in the work. Seeing lives transformed, and getting a front-row seat to the Holy Spirit's work, is a far superior pleasure than any of our sins! Jesus' mission is invigorating.

****

I pray that God empowers you with the gospel to implement these strategies in your life, and that God blesses your repentance to give you greater joy in Jesus and victory over sin.

CONCLUSION: THE END OF THE FIGHT

"When we shall come home and enter to the possession of our Brother's fair kingdom, and when our heads shall find the weight of the eternal crown of glory, and when we shall look back to pains and sufferings; then shall we see life and sorrow to be less than one step or stride from a prison to glory; and that our little inch of time — suffering is not worthy of our first night's welcome home to heaven." – Samuel Rutherford, The Loveliness of Christ[40]

****

There will be an end to the fight. The relentless fight against besetting sins does not last forever, and this is gloriously good news! I want to finish this short book with a final encouragement about how God will bring His work of salvation to completion. If you're a Christian, the last word in your life will be victory in Jesus.

Meditate on these comforting promises that God gives:

- ❖ John 6:39, "And this is the will of him who sent me, that I should lose nothing of all that he has given me, but raise it up on the last day."
- ❖ Romans 16:20, "The God of peace will soon crush Satan under your feet. The grace of our Lord Jesus Christ be with you."
- ❖ 1 Corinthians 1:7b-9, "...as you wait for the revealing of our Lord Jesus Christ, who will sustain you to the end, guiltless in the day of our Lord Jesus Christ. God is faithful, by whom you

were called into the fellowship of his Son, Jesus Christ our Lord."

❖ Philippians 1:6, "And I am sure of this, that he who began a good work in you will bring it to completion at the day of Jesus Christ."

❖ 1 Thessalonians 5:23-24, "Now may the God of peace himself sanctify you completely, and may your whole spirit and soul and body be kept blameless at the coming of our Lord Jesus Christ. He who calls you is faithful; he will surely do it."

❖ Jude 1:24-25, "Now to him who is able to keep you from stumbling and to present you blameless before the presence of his glory with great joy, to the only God, our Savior, through Jesus Christ our Lord, be glory, majesty, dominion, and authority, before all time and now and forever. Amen."

What can we learn from these glorious truths? How does this give us comfort and confidence, as we fight the battles against sin?

God is the One who has started this work of salvation. So it doesn't all depend on us. He began it, He will continue it, and He will bring it to completion. Our salvation is *His* idea, it is *His* plan. This relieves the pressure on us, and puts the pressure back on God. He can bear that burden which otherwise would crush us. Trust Him to bring His work in your life to completion. Trust Him like you would a firefighter carrying you out of a burning building.

Notice also that God is committed to our perseverance. He will not give up, and He will present us blameless before His presence! He will render us guiltless. He will *not* lose us. Look at God's commitment to you! Be confident in this, especially when doubts begin to rise, and Satan speaks words of discouragement to your heart. God does *not* break His promises. What He purposes, He accomplishes.

Scripture tells us that the end is *near* and the victory is *sure*. It's close and it's secure. You won't have to wait very long, and you don't have to worry that it will fail. The God of peace will *soon* crush Satan under your feet (Romans 16:20). In addition, there's no danger that God will not succeed. He will ultimately be victorious over our sin, and He will finish the fight. Granted, it might not be in our lifetime, but it surely is coming. The saints of old in Hebrews 11 died in faith, waiting for the promise. They sit in the stands, cheering you on as you fight the same great fight of faith! Hebrews 12:1-2 concludes, "Therefore, since we are surrounded by so great a cloud of witnesses, let us also lay aside every weight, and sin which clings so closely, and let us run with endurance the race that is set before us, looking to Jesus, the founder and perfecter of our faith, who for the joy that was set before him endured the cross, despising the shame, and is seated at the right hand of the throne of God." Look to Jesus, and receive endurance.

There's an old song I remember as a child, singing at Sunday School. It goes, "We win, we win, hallelujah we win. I've read the back of the book, and we win!"[41] That's our confidence as Christians. Our God knows the beginning, middle, and end of the story. He has shown us the end of the story... and we win! Satan is defeated. Sin is wiped away. We are in God's presence, and death is no more. There is no more failure. No more guilt. No more shame. These are old things that have passed away! We have full joy in Jesus. We are healed. Addictions are broken, stains are gone, and all the suffering and fighting will be worth it. Yes, we labor and fight and toil in this life on earth, but in heaven we shall see that our labor was not in vain. In heaven we shall see the fruit of our fight. We shall rejoice in God our Savior, and see Him face to face. We will all sing and dance at the great victory party, as we praise Jesus for conquering Satan, sin, and death. We win, we win, hallelujah we win!

Let this vision of heaven invigorate you for the fight against sin. You are engaged in battle with a defeated foe. This should give you confidence, and this must spur you on in endurance. Keep fighting, because your hope of heaven is secure. Stay in the battle, because your King rules and reigns. You have solid hope in Jesus. It's not up in the air whether your efforts will be effective. It's not a question of *if* you will ultimately win. No, our victory is secure in Christ.

As our final word, listen to this glorious future in store for us from Revelation 21:3-5, "And I heard a loud voice from the throne saying, 'Behold, the dwelling place of God is with man. He will dwell with them, and they will be his people, and God himself will be with them as their God. He will wipe away every tear from their eyes, and death shall be no more, neither shall there be mourning, nor crying, nor pain anymore, for the former things have passed away.' And he who was seated on the throne said, 'Behold, I am making all things new.' Also he said, 'Write this down, for these words are trustworthy and true.'"

APPENDIX A: WHAT TO DO AFTER A FAILURE

Let's be real.... You are going to fail. Reading this book isn't a quick fix. There is no perfection in the Christian life. It's a fight. The Christian life is a hard, long, bloody fight.[42]

So what do you do when you fail? I want to give you a slow-motion breakdown of how you should respond to your next failure.

The next time you fail, you need to Confess, Repent, Believe, Rejoice, and Fight.[43] Let's break it down for each of these five steps:

1. Confess: The very first step is to admit to God what you have just done. Be direct and clear: "I have sinned." This starts the whole repentance process from a place of humility and honesty. It's best if you can use biblical language to describe your sin: anger, pride, unbelief, idolatry, lust. Don't downplay the sin by using slang like "We had an affair," or a vague allusion like, "I messed up." Name the sin, and accept the guilt. Confession to God is most important, but confession to other Christians will bring many benefits. Sin thrives in secret, so one of the first ways to start killing sin is to drag it out into the light with God and others. If you are unwilling to confess your sin, you are unwilling to fight your sin, and you are unable to believe the gospel. Only confessed sinners are eligible for forgiveness through the cross. Confession is the first step, and it is utterly necessary.

2. Repent: As you confess your sin, you must turn away from it. Repentance means a change in mind, heart, and behavior. You break your promise with your sin, you cancel your contract, you betray your love, and you reverse your trajectory. Repentance is the heart of the Christian life; it is the means of spiritual growth. If you are unwilling to repent, it means you love your sin more than you love your Savior. It is a refusal to change.

3. Believe: Remember the gospel and believe it! Believe that it is *true*. Recount to yourself the massive promises found in Jesus' salvation for sinners. Remember that you are a new creation in Christ (2 Corinthians 5:17). Remember that Jesus has cleaned away your shame (1 John 1:7). Remember that your guilt is atoned for (1 Corinthians 1:8). Remember that you are forgiven (Acts 10:43). Believe this good news! Shout it out loud, sing it, write it down, pray it, ask someone to speak it to you. Do not forget it.

4. Rejoice: This is a crucial step. Do not stop at mere intellectual belief in the gospel. You must *rejoice*! Get excited, get happy, let the joy of the good news dwell in you richly (Colossians 3:16). This is a fight in itself, because in your sin you feel guilty and ashamed and discouraged. But if you really remembered and believed the gospel, you would rejoice! *Thank* God for the gospel, choose gratitude. Sing, shout, smile, jump up and down if you have to. Keep coming back to the gospel, believing it, meditating on it, until the joy fills your soul. A refusal to rejoice means the gospel has not really entered your heart; you are still stuck in discouragement and lies.

5. Fight: In the joy of the gospel, you will have fresh motivation to fight your sin. You probably know what next steps to take. Pick up your sword and get back into the fray. Maybe there are some lessons to be learned from this most recent failure. Maybe you realize you need specific help from other Christians. Maybe you need to memorize some truth in Scripture to combat the lies of temptation. Maybe you need to set up better strategies to avoid situations where you are vulnerable. Whatever it looks like to fight, *do it.*

That's how to respond immediately after a failure: confess, repent, believe, rejoice, and fight. Start with confession as *soon* as possible after a failure; don't delay a week, a day, an hour, or even one minute. And it doesn't need to take long to go through these five steps! This process of responding to a failure can be fast, taking only a few minutes. Or you can intentionally move slowly as you journal and pray, taking as long as you need. The purpose isn't to get through it quickly, but to go through it deliberately. Don't skip any of the steps! Don't attempt to go from confession to fighting without the power of the gospel.

While the response to one sin can be quick, the response to *all* the sins of one's life will be slow. The process of real lasting change is often grueling, taking years. Please realize that redemption comes slowly. If you have a false view of the speed of sanctification, you'll get disenchanted and give up too soon. Don't think the fight will be short or easy or clean. It's not a simple victory. You'll go through these five responses again and again, probably hundreds of times. But the gospel is powerful and will give you the endurance and power to slowly change. The Holy Spirit can and does bring victory!

Focus on the *direction*, not the speed, of your sanctification.[44] Celebrate small progress! Zoom out the lens to better see God's work in you, and ask the powerful question, "How am I different than a year ago?" or ask a close friend to share with you evidences of God's work in your life.

All of life is repentance. And that makes for a life of fighting. What will keep you going, especially when you fail? Answer: the *gospel*. The power of the gospel gives motivation for the fight against sin. If you forget the gospel, you will stop fighting. If you forget that you've been forgiven, you'll wallow in guilt. If you forget that you've been cleansed, you'll be shackled by shame and too broken to fight. If you forget that you are *loved* by God, you'll try to look for love in the wrong places. If you forget the power of God's Word given to you, you'll never pick up the sword of the Scripture.

So remember the gospel, and keep fighting.

APPENDIX B: HOW CAN YOU HELP OTHERS?

The hope of the gospel not only motivates you to fight your sin, it excites you to share this hope with others! There are other struggling sinners in need of the same encouragement that you have received. They need the power of the gospel. They require tools for the fight against sin. Now that you have encouragement, empowerment, and equipping... how can you help others?

One of my greatest joys in college ministry is helping young students to know the power of the gospel and effectively fight their sin. It is so exciting to have a front row seat to see God's work of transforming change in their lives! You too can experience this great joy as you help others.

There are three steps to helping others,[45] namely: *listen*, *remind*, and *help* them. These three responses can also be categorized as encourage, empower, and equip. You will generally do them in this order, but all three aspects will be present as you care for people:

I. Listen (Encourage): Listen to the people you are seeking to help. This may seem "soft" or impractical, but it's probably the best way to love people. Seek to understand how they are feeling, and ask deeper questions to unearth what they're struggling with and how it's affecting them. Some example questions: "How are you doing? What are you going through? What is most difficult in this? How are you feeling? What has been helpful? What have you already tried? How can I help you? How can I pray for you?" Listen and ask more questions. Repeat back to them a summary to make sure you understand them correctly. Try to see their struggle from their point of view, and put yourself in their shoes. Linger on this step of listening, and ideally you will begin to be emotionally affected as you move to empathy. God listens to us in our prayers, so we want to listen to others. Pray that God helps you to listen well.

2. Remind (Empower): Remind them of the gospel. Speak it with power and authority. Speak it with joy. Perhaps go to a specific Scripture like 1 Corinthians 15:1-4 or Titus 3:3-7 or even the classic John 3:16. Evangelism is not just for unbelievers; Christians need to be reminded of the gospel often! And since you've already listened well, you can connect to the specifics of their situation with relevant aspects of the gospel. If they're feeling guilt, you can speak of Christ's forgiveness. If they're feeling rejected, you can speak of Christ's acceptance. If they're feeling like they'll never change, you can speak of how God has made them a new creation in Christ and is committed to their growth by His Spirit. Pray that God would remind them of the gospel and give them fresh faith to believe it. Pray that God restores to them the joy of their salvation (Psalm 51:12).

3. Help (Equip): Help them in this fight! Once they're encouraged and empowered by the gospel, it's time for them to get back into the fight against sin. Equip them. Give them strategies and tactics and weapons and tools and resources. What do they need? How can you help? Do they need accountability and check-ins? Do they need help identifying where their battlefield of temptation is?

Do they need to memorize Scripture? Would it be helpful to read through a book together with them? What are practical steps of putting off their sin and putting on holiness? How can you help them? Ask them questions to discern what would best equip them. Pray for the Spirit to energize their efforts at sanctification.

Finally, **pray**. This isn't a distinct step in the process, because you should be praying for other people throughout your relationship with them. Your ministry should be soaked in prayer and love. Practically, it may be helpful to pray briefly in the beginning of your conversation, and to pray more specifically at the end of your conversation. Follow up later on what you prayed about, and ask them how God has been at work, and how you can pray for them again. Praying for other people *is* ministry.[46] And pray for yourself; pray that God gives you wisdom and humility to care well for them. Pray that God gives you words that encourage them and point them to Jesus. Pray that God gives you endurance in walking with them.

As you help more people, it'll give you joy in two ways: First, you will get a front-row seat to seeing God's work in changing this person. How exciting! It is exhilarating to see someone's steps of growth as the Spirit is on the move. Second, you'll see how God is redeeming your own struggles (even if they aren't the same category as this person, but especially if it's the same struggle) because you'll be able to share with them the same gospel that has transformed your life. You'll be able to empathize with them in their struggle, because you know your own struggle. You'll be able to share practical strategies that have helped you, so they can be helped too. You'll see how God breaks the power of your own sin, and turns it on its head as you help to rescue others.

I pray that God motivates you to help other people! As more and more Christians move toward each other, we will constantly reinvigorate one another in the power of the gospel and strength to fight our sin. This gives us much joy, and brings God much glory!

APPENDIX C: BIBLIOGRAPHY & FURTHER READING

This book is intentionally short, because if you are a discouraged sinner, you need encouragement quickly. You may not have the emotional or spiritual energy right now to be reading hundreds of pages. But if this book has infused you with some hope, some gospel encouragement, and some of the Spirit's power (and I pray it has!) then perhaps you'd like to dig deeper into some more weighty truth and strategies. Obviously the Scriptures will be your most powerful resource. Above any of these listed resources, I encourage you to read the Word. Read slowly verse by verse, read quickly through whole books in one sitting, read in groups for discussion, and read in private study. Read the Bible however you would like, but above all, read the Word.

After you've gorged yourself on the Bible, perhaps you'd like some other weapons for the fight. Enjoy this library.

Bibliography:

* ❖ *The Holy Bible: English Standard Version: The ESV Study Bible* (Wheaton, IL: Crossway Bibles, 2008)
* ❖ John Owen, edited by Kelly M. Kapic and Justin Taylor, *Overcoming Sin and Temptation* (Wheaton, IL: Crossway Books, 2006) Note: This edition features three of Owen's works. I've drawn from "Of the Mortification of Sin in Believers," which is more

commonly referred to as "The Mortification of Sin" in updated or abridged versions.

❖ John Piper and Justin Taylor, *Sex and the Supremacy of Christ* (Wheaton, IL: Crossway Books, 2005)

❖ Tim Chester, *Closing the Window: Steps to Living Porn Free* (Downers Grove, IL: InterVarsity Press, 2010)

Resources on the Gospel:

❖ *Death by Love: Letters from the Cross* by Mark Driscoll

❖ *Desiring God: Meditations of a Christian Hedonist* by John Piper

❖ *Gospel-Centered Discipleship* by Jonathan K. Dodson

❖ Global Missions: there are so many good organizations! To start, check out www.thetravelingteam.org and www.JoshuaProject.net

❖ *Spiritual Depression: Its Causes and Its Cure* by David Martyn Lloyd-Jones

❖ *The Cross-Centered Life: Keeping the Gospel the Main Thing* by CJ Mahaney

❖ *The Explicit Gospel* by Matt Chandler

❖ *The Discipline of Grace: God's Role and Our Role in the Pursuit of Holiness* by Jerry Bridges

❖ *The Hole in our Holiness: Filling the Gap between Gospel Passion and the Pursuit of Godliness* by Kevin DeYoung

❖ *What is the Gospel?* by Greg Gilbert

❖ *When I Don't Desire God: How to Fight for Joy* by John Piper. Book review on The Relentless Fight blog: https://therelentlessfight.blogspot.com/2014/09/when-i-dont-desire-god.html

❖ "How to Deal with the Guilt of Sexual Failure for the Glory of Christ and His Global Cause" sermon by John Piper: http://www.desiringgod.org/resource-library/conference-messages/how-to-deal-with-the-guilt-of-sexual-failure-for-the-glory-of-christ-and-his-global-cause

Resources on Fighting Sin:

❖ *12 Ways Your Phone is Changing You* by Tony Reinke. Book review on The Relentless Fight blog: https://therelentlessfight.blogspot.com/2017/08/book-review-12-ways-your-phone-is.html

❖ ANTHEM article by John Piper: https://www.desiringgod.org/articles/anthem-strategies-for-fighting-lust

❖ CCEF (Christian Counseling and Education Foundation): www.ccef.org

❖ *Closing the Window: Steps to Living Porn Free* by Tim Chester

❖ *Caring for One Another: 8 Ways to Cultivate Meaningful Relationships* by Ed Welch. Book review on The Relentless Fight blog: https://therelentlessfight.blogspot.com/2018/07/book-review-caring-for-one-another.html

❖ *How Does Sanctification Work?* by David Powlison. Book review on The Relentless Fight blog: https://therelentlessfight.blogspot.com/2017/10/book-review-how-does-sanctification-work.html

- ❖ *How People Change* by Tim Lane and Paul David Tripp
- ❖ *Habits of Grace: Enjoying Jesus through the Spiritual Disciplines* by David Mathis
- ❖ Internet filters & accountability: there's so many out there. Some to consider: X3watch, Covenant Eyes, Curbi, Accountable2You, and OpenDNS.
- ❖ *Love to Eat, Hate to Eat: Breaking the Bondage of Destructive Eating Habits* by Elyse Fitzpatrick. Book review on The Relentless Fight blog: https://therelentlessfight.blogspot.com/2013/07/love-to-eat-hate-to-eat.html
- ❖ *Precious Remedies Against Satan's Devices* by Thomas Brooks. Book review on The Relentless Fight blog: https://therelentlessfight.blogspot.com/2012/08/precious-remedies-against-satans-devices.html
- ❖ *Sex and the Supremacy of Christ* edited by John Piper and Justin Taylor. The book contains edited transcripts of the sessions from the 2004 Desiring God National Conference. The audio recordings can be listened to on Desiring God: https://www.desiringgod.org/series/2004-national-conference
- ❖ *Sex is Not the Problem (Lust Is): Sexual Purity in a Lust-Saturated World* by Joshua Harris. Book review on The Relentless Fight blog: https://therelentlessfight.blogspot.com/2014/03/sex-is-not-problem-lust-is.html
- ❖ *Sexual Sanity for Men: Re-creating Your Mind in a Crazy Culture* by David White. Book review on The Relentless Fight blog:

https://therelentlessfight.blogspot.com/2013/04/sexual-sanity-for-men.html There's also a companion book for women: *Sexual Sanity for Women: Healing from Sexual and Relational Brokenness* by Ellen Dykas

❖ *Side by Side: Walking with Others in Wisdom and Love* by Ed Welch. Book review on The Relentless Fight blog: https://therelentlessfight.blogspot.com/2016/05/side-by-side.html

❖ *Tap: Defeating The Sins That Defeat You* by Yancey Arrington

❖ *The Great Divorce* by C. S. Lewis

❖ The *Mortification of Sin* by John Owen. There are many editions of this 1656 classic, but I suggest the compilation of three of Owen's works titled *Overcoming Sin & Temptation*, edited by Kelly M. Kapic and Justin Taylor. Book review on The Relentless Fight blog: https://therelentlessfight.blogspot.com/2015/06/of-mortification-of-sin-in-believers.html

❖ *The Screwtape Letters* by C. S. Lewis

❖ *You Can Change: God's Transforming Power for Our Sinful Behavior and Negative Emotions* by Tim Chester

❖ "The Fight" 3-part sermon series by Ben Stuart: https://www.tvcresources.net/resource-library/sermons/by-series/the-fight

❖ Fight the New Drug, a non-religious organization raising awareness of the harmful effects of pornography: www.fightthenewdrug.org

❖ Online accountability groups for porn addiction recovery: Conquer Series: https://conquerseries.com/, Freedom Fight: https://thefreedomfight.org/, Setting Captives Free: https://settingcaptivesfree.com/, and many others.

ACKNOWLEDGMENTS & ABOUT THE AUTHOR

Acknowledgments

Praise and honor must first and supremely go to God: the Father, Son, and Spirit for the work of salvation in my life, and for empowering my very breath. Thank you for the gospel. You receive all glory.

Gratitude and honor must also go to a number of people. I need to humbly recognize that I'm standing on the shoulders of many others.

Melissa: you're the best! Thanks for joining me on this adventure of life as my wife, ministry partner, mother to our children, and best friend. Thanks for supporting and encouraging my work on this book, and being a frequent sounding board for all my ideas.

Mom & Dad (Suzy & John Cimbala): thank you for being the first people to introduce me to Jesus. Thank you for telling me the gospel and laying a firm foundation of Biblical truth for my life; you are wonderful parents. Mom, thanks for your many sacrifices to help me grow and succeed. Dad, seeing you self-publish your novels on Amazon and holding those books in my hands made me think, "Hey, maybe I could do that too!"

My brother Luke: thanks for being so excited when I first told you my idea for this book years ago!

Phil Miller: the challenge you issued for our "production time" was a key catalyst for this book making progress and coming to completion.

Dave White: the Lord has used you in my life in significant ways. I'm so grateful for your wisdom and encouragement in helping me in the fight for sexual purity.

DiscipleMakers: the college ministry that God used when I was at Penn State to greatly transform my life. I was so impacted during my time in college that I joined their staff! Thank you to the many Bible teachers, disciplers, and friends for whom I owe most of my growth. The Lord has used you all in immense ways to make me the disciple of Jesus and disciple maker that I am today. Extra thanks to David Royes, Joel Martin, Gary Brown, Tom Hallman, Dave Kieffer, and Ben Hagerup.

Brothers in Arms: thank you to the many faithful bros who have walked with me in the fight, prayed for my growth, and given me encouragement when desperately needed.

John Cimbala, Sarah Dorrance, Peter Krol, Mark Fodale, Phil Miller, and Ben Hagerup: thank you for reading over the very first draft and giving initial feedback. Dan Miller, Brian Roberg, Caleb Olshefsky, and Jordan Eyster: thank you for sharing your expert artistic feedback on the cover designs.

Proverbs 15:22 says, "Without counsel plans fail, but with many advisers they succeed." There was an abundance of counselors on this book project! Thank you to the many helpful readers and editors of the manuscript: John Cimbala (again, with a keen eye for grammar!), Mark Campbell, Melissa Cimbala, Matthew Bryant, Bob Rudge, Chase Abner, Paul Worcester, Maria Noyes, Nate Powles, Luke Cimbala, Rashard Barnes, Madi Wenger, Tanner Callison, Peter Krol, Tom Hallman, Janáe

Siford (twice!), Lincoln Fitch, Dave Kraft, Christa Luckenbach, Jenny Fitch, James Osinski, Steve Shadrach, Mike Kreider, Felicia Gater, Tim Casteel, Josiah Kennealy, Kyle Bushre, Mike Puckett, Antonio Morton, Andrew Maple, Dave Kieffer, and Curtis Dunlap. This book was significantly improved because of your partnership, thank you.

John Piper, John Owen, Tim Chester, Ben Stuart, Martyn Lloyd-Jones, Greg Gilbert, Mark Driscoll, Joshua Harris, C. S. Lewis, Jerry Bridges, and David Powlison: I'm grateful for your teaching, writing, and investment into my life. You don't know me, but the Lord has used you greatly. Thank you.

About the Author

Andy Cimbala and his wife Melissa have a passion to make disciples of college students. They work with DiscipleMakers, leading Bible studies and mentoring leaders. You can contact Andy here: www.dm.org/andy-melissa-cimbala

The Relentless Fight blog exists to encourage, empower, and equip Christians for the great fight of faith. You can follow updates on social media and read here: www.therelentlessfight.blogspot.com

ENDNOTES

1 John Owen, edited by Kelly M. Kapic and Justin Taylor, *Overcoming Sin and Temptation* (Wheaton, IL: Crossway Books, 2006), page 50.

2 "Fight the New Drug," accessed January 5, 2019, https://www.fightthenewdrug.org/

3 For more texts on a biblical sexual ethic, please read: Exodus 20:14, Proverbs 5-7, 1 Corinthians 5-7, Ephesians 5:1-12, and 1 Thessalonians 4:1-11, among others.

4 C. S. Lewis describes this tension and wrestling perfectly in his book *The Great Divorce*: A man from hell is visiting heaven, and has the opportunity to stay in heaven, but it means repenting from his sexual lust, which is incarnated as a small red lizard. He greatly fears the loss of even his own life if the lizard is to die. But he cannot stay in heaven with the lizard. He must choose. (I distinctly remember reading this section in fall semester 2006, and it jumped off the page at me.)

5 This book was later re-released and re-titled as *Sex Is Not the Problem (Lust Is): Sexual Purity in a Lust-Saturated World*. Both are authored by Joshua Harris.

6 The breaking down of Asherah poles and Baal altars was the quintessential act of repentance in pre-exilic Israel. Examples include Judges 6:25f, 1 Kings 15:13, 2 Kings 10:26f, 11:18, and 18:4.

7 John Piper, "Sex and the Supremacy of Christ Part 2," Desiring God, accessed January 5, 2019, https://www.desiringgod.org/messages/sex-and-the-supremacy-of-christ-part-2

8 John Piper, "Sex and the Supremacy of Christ Part 2," Desiring God, accessed January 5, 2019, https://www.desiringgod.org/messages/sex-and-the-supremacy-of-christ-part-2

9 What do you expect in the fight against sin? For more on this, read "Expect a Hard Long Bloody Fight" on The Relentless Fight

blog: https://therelentlessfight.blogspot.com/2013/07/expect-hard-long-bloody-fight.html

[10] C. S. Lewis makes this profound point in the words of the demon Screwtape: "You will say that these are very small sins; and doubtless, like all young tempters, you are anxious to be able to report spectacular wickedness. But do remember, the only thing that matters is the extent to which you separate the man from the Enemy. It does not matter how small the sins are provided that their cumulative effect is to edge the man away from the Light and out into the Nothing. Murder is no better than cards if cards can do the trick. Indeed the safest road to Hell is the gradual one—the general slope, soft underfoot, without sudden turnings, without milestones, without signposts..." C. S. Lewis, *Screwtape Letters* (New York: Harper Collins, 2001), page 60-61.

[11] John Owen, edited by Kelly M. Kapic and Justin Taylor, *Overcoming Sin and Temptation* (Wheaton, IL: Crossway Books, 2006), page 131.

[12] John Piper, *When I Don't Desire God: How to Fight for Joy* (Wheaton, IL: Crossway Books, 2004), page 81.

[13] John Piper calls this "gutsy guilt" and he uses Micah 7 as a text in this fantastic sermon: "How to Deal with the Guilt of Sexual Failure for the Glory of Christ and His Global Cause" http://www.desiringgod.org/resource-library/conference-messages/how-to-deal-with-the-guilt-of-sexual-failure-for-the-glory-of-christ-and-his-global-cause

[14] "Do you find your corruption to begin to entangle your thoughts? Rise up with all your strength against it, with no less indignation than if it had fully accomplished what it aims at. Consider what an unclean thought would have; it would have you roll yourself in folly and filth. Ask envy what it would have—murder and destruction is at the end of it. Set yourself against it with no less vigor than if it had utterly debased you to wickedness. Without this course you will not prevail. As sin gets ground in the affections to delight in, it gets also upon the

understanding to slight it." John Owen, edited by Kelly M. Kapic and Justin Taylor, *Overcoming Sin and Temptation* (Wheaton, IL: Crossway Books, 2006), page 110.

[15] John Owen, edited by Kelly M. Kapic and Justin Taylor, *Overcoming Sin and Temptation* (Wheaton, IL: Crossway Books, 2006), page 88.

[16] Only sinners are eligible for the gospel! Only those who confess their wickedness will receive forgiveness. Only those who hunger and thirst for righteousness (because they have none of their own) will be satisfied. Remember Luke 18:9-14, Jesus tells the parable of the Pharisee and the tax collector. Which one went down to his house justified?

[17] For more on this "effort" of faith, read *Spiritual Depression: Its Causes and Its Cure* by D. Martyn Lloyd-Jones and *When I Don't Desire God: How to Fight for Joy* by John Piper.

[18] Thousands of John Piper's sermons, videos, podcasts, and articles can be found at Desiring God: https://www.desiringgod.org/

[19] Timothy S. Lane, Paul David Tripp, *How People Change* (New Growth Press, 2006), page 187.

[20] Nathan W. Bingham and R. C. Sproul, "What Does "Simul Justus et Peccator" Mean?," Ligonier Ministries, accessed January 16, 2019, https://www.ligonier.org/blog/simul-justus-et-peccator/

[21] John Owen, edited by Kelly M. Kapic and Justin Taylor, *Overcoming Sin and Temptation* (Wheaton, IL: Crossway Books, 2006), page 52.

[22] John Owen, edited by Kelly M. Kapic and Justin Taylor, *Overcoming Sin and Temptation* (Wheaton, IL: Crossway Books, 2006), page 47.

[23] John Owen, edited by Kelly M. Kapic and Justin Taylor, *Overcoming Sin and Temptation* (Wheaton, IL: Crossway Books, 2006), page 133.

[24] David Powlison, "Making All Things New: Restoring Pure Joy to the Sexually Broken," Desiring God, accessed January 5,

2019, https://www.desiringgod.org/messages/making-all-things-new-restoring-pure-joy-to-the-sexually-broken

[25] Ben Stuart, "The War Room," time mark 12:32, The Village Church, accessed January 6, 2019, https://www.tvcresources.net/resource-library/sermons/the-war-room

[26] It's generally wise to share about sexual sins only with same-gender Christians. Don't be that freshman guy who foolishly talks with a lady in your Christian fellowship about your struggle with lust. Don't post it on social media for all to see. Pursue older wiser Christians (privately) who can walk with you and help you grow.

[27] There are a host of helpful online support groups, especially for fighting sexual addiction. Consider Conquer Series: https://conquerseries.com/, Freedom Fight: https://thefreedomfight.org/, Setting Captives Free: https://settingcaptivesfree.com/, and many others.

[28] Richard Baxter, *Christian Directory* (London: Robert White, 1673), pages 398-401. Quoted by Mark Dever, "Christian Hedonists or Religious Prudes? The Puritans on Sex," in *Sex and Supremacy of Christ* (Wheaton, IL: Crossway Books, 2005), page 260.

[29] Paul Worcester, "Whatever It Takes: Helping Your Students and Yourself Gain Freedom from Lust and Porn," Faith On Campus, accessed January 5, 2019, http://faithoncampus.com/blog/whatever-it-takes-helping-your-students-and-yourself-gain-freedom-from-lust-and-porn/

[30] E.V. Hill, "How to Make the Enemy Run," GodTube, accessed January 7, 2019, https://www.godtube.com/watch/?v=7PKKWNNX Note: The video clip says this message was originally presented at a 1993 PromiseKeepers event. I could not find a full recording or more information on the PK website as the provided link was broken,

but here's the organization's current website: https://promisekeepers.org

[31] Joshua Harris, *Sex is Not the Problem (Lust Is): Sexual Purity in a Lust-Saturated World* (Colorado Spring, CO: Multnomah Books, 2003), page 158-159

[32] I've drawn inspiration for this section from Tim Chester, Chapter 2 "Freed by the Beauty of God," *Closing the Window: Steps to Living Porn Free* (Downers Grove, IL: InterVarsity Press, 2010), pages 37-65.

[33] John Piper, "What's the Origin of Desiring God's Slogan?" Desiring God, accessed January 5, 2019, https://www.desiringgod.org/interviews/whats-the-origin-of-desiring-gods-slogan

[34] Ben Stuart, "Practical Helps for Bible Reading," YouTube, accessed February 4, 2019, https://www.youtube.com/watch?v=_RaejuYkh-M

[35] For more on this, read "Relentless Prayer" on The Relentless Fight blog: https://therelentlessfight.blogspot.com/2017/07/relentless-prayer.html

[36] John Piper, "Fighting Porn Addiction with Grudem's Systematic Theology," Desiring God, accessed January 5, 2019, https://www.desiringgod.org/interviews/fighting-porn-addiction-with-grudems-systematic-theology

[37] For more on this, read "Force Feed Yourself the Word" on The Relentless Fight blog: https://therelentlessfight.blogspot.com/2013/05/force-feed-yourself-word.html

[38] "Definitions," Joshua Project, accessed January 5, 2019, https://joshuaproject.net/help/definitions

[39] David Mathis, *Habits of Grace: Enjoying Jesus Through the Spiritual Disciplines* (Wheaton, IL: Crossway Books, 2016), page 198.

[40] Samuel Rutherford, *The Loveliness of Christ: Extracts from the Letters of Samuel Rutherford* (East Peoria, IL: Banner of Truth Trust, 2009), page 19.

[41] My memory might not serve me accurately, but perhaps the song I'm thinking of is :"I've Read the Back of the Book and We Win."

[42] For more on this, read "Expect a Hard Long Bloody Fight" on The Relentless Fight blog:

https://therelentlessfight.blogspot.com/2013/07/expect-hard-long-bloody-fight.html

[43] Appendix A is adapted from "Right After the Failure" on The Relentless Fight blog:

https://therelentlessfight.blogspot.com/2013/06/right-after-failure.html

[44] "First, sanctification is a direction in which you are heading." David Powlison, "Making All Things New: Restoring Pure Joy to the Sexually Broken," Desiring God, accessed January 5, 2019, https://www.desiringgod.org/messages/making-all-things-new-restoring-pure-joy-to-the-sexually-broken

[45] Appendix B is adapted from "3 Steps in Ministering to Others" on The Relentless Fight blog:

https://therelentlessfight.blogspot.com/2014/06/3-steps-in-ministering-to-others.html

[46] "Knowing others well enough to pray for them—that's help at its most basic and at its best." Edward T. Welch, *Side by Side: Walking with Others in Wisdom and Love* (Wheaton, IL: Crossway Books, 2015), page 84.

Made in the USA
Middletown, DE
23 March 2019